The
Incarnation

with thanks
for your
appreciation.

Tom

The Incarnation

Finding Our True Self Through Christ

First published by Floris Books in 2014

British Library CIP Data available
ISBN 978-178250-060-5
Printed in Great Britain,
by DS Smith Print Solutions, Glasgow

Contents

To Ormond Edwards in gratitude

He who was the Son of God became the Son of man, that man, having been taken into the Word, and receiving the adoption, might become the son of God.

Irenaeus, Adv. Haer, *II 19.1*

Introduction

I am all at once what Christ is, for he was what I am.

G. M. Hopkins

The Incarnation of the Son of God in Jesus Christ is at the heart of Christian experience. This book offers a pathway to a deeper understanding of how the Incarnation came about and how it changed human possibilities. This seems important in a world in which the cleft widens between those who seek the spirit as the opposite of the world of the senses and those who deny the spirit and see in the sense-world the explanation for all of our experiences. Understanding and experiencing the Incarnation opens up the possibility of saying yes to our experiences on the earth whilst finding a new connection to the spiritual world.

The first chapter explores how knowledge of Christ could be possible. Chapter 2 is about the awareness of the divided world that underlies the need for the Incarnation. Chapters 3 and 4 trace some of the major stages on the journey towards understanding the Incarnation in the first five centuries of the Church, culminating in the Council of Chalcedon (451). Understanding the struggles of the early theologians to grasp the Incarnation can school our own thinking.

Chapters 5 and 6 explore a new possibility of thinking about the Incarnation today, drawing on the methods and research results shared by Rudolf Steiner (1861–1925). Steiner was uniquely equipped to understand the Incarnation, as his life's work was devoted to showing that the world is really one. He brought a huge array of insights into the Incarnation from a diverse range of points of view.

The final chapter turns to the question of how the fact that

God became man in Jesus Christ makes it possible for us to find out true self.

Although this book describes a path of thinking, it is not intended to convince its readers by the force of logical argument. Its aim is to stimulate thought and further reflection. For this reason, throughout the book there are 'Contemplations' that relate to the content. Inspired by Rudolf Steiner's instructions on the inner life, they are intended as examples of how we could bring what is discussed to life within us.

1. Knowing Christ

And the Word became flesh and made his dwelling amongst us, and
we have beheld his glory, the glory of the only-begotten of the Father.

John 1:14

Because the heart of Christianity is a relationship with Jesus
Christ, Christian theology has always been more than intellectual
study. It is a quest to know Christ as intimately as our closest
friend.

The first question that the early Christian theologians faced
was: who was Jesus Christ? To begin with, the answers to this
question represented extreme positions. Some of the first followers
of Christ said that he was just a man – one of the long line of
prophets, or the long-awaited Messiah, God's Anointed. This
earthly king would be given the honour of being 'adopted' as
God's son once he had restored the kingdom of Israel, as David
had been adopted at his coronation. Others said that he was
indeed God, but that it was absurd to say that God could become
human. These extremes were eventually overcome through the
insight that Jesus Christ united humanity and divinity within
himself.

The second great question arose from this insight: how can we
imagine God becoming human? The different emphases on the
human and the divine remained, now transposed within the God-
man. One school of thought focused on the man whose striving
made him worthy of being united with the God; the other turned
its gaze to the descent of the divine Word as he entered human
nature – his 'flesh'. In 451 the debates were brought to a climax
and a preliminary conclusion at the Council of Chalcedon. The
movement between the extremes is frozen in the paradoxical
description: *Vere deus, vere homo* – 'truly God and truly man'.

When we think of the God-man, we must not confuse the divine and the human, but we also must not divide them in two. They cannot be thought of as separate, but they may not be merged into one.

The Definition of Chalcedon has stood as a touchstone of right belief in mainstream Christianity for sixteen centuries. It gives a conceptual framework for thinking the Incarnation when it says that a human and a divine nature come together in one 'person' without being merged into something new, but without being able to drift apart again. But the Definition offers little help if we wish to allow the reality of the Incarnation to come alive in our souls. Friedrich Schleiermacher (1768–1834), often seen as the father of modern liberal theology, said that the Definition of Chalcedon never made anyone pious. A child of the Romantic period, Schleiermacher was concerned to anchor Christianity in the realm of feeling, the very opposite of the dry abstractions that he saw in the Definition. Perhaps it is not surprising that today, the Definition of Chalcedon is largely neglected. Speculation about the mechanics of the Incarnation seems absurd to an age for which the events recorded in the Gospels are hardly more than a myth.

Rudolf Steiner's insights into the development of consciousness can help us to understand the achievement of the first five centuries of Christianity. For Steiner, changes in our way of thinking are not merely the product of material culture or the outer transmission of ideas, but they emerge from a journey on which human beings are coming of age. When children pass from a mythic consciousness to logical thinking, they are repeating the journey of humanity. The fourth century was a time of transition in which mythological thinking was growing weak. Logic and rational argument took the place of mystical experience. We can see the Definition of Chalcedon as the crowning achievement of Christian thinking, which distills into abstract concepts what could no longer be experienced so immediately. Rudolf Steiner shows us how to develop a way of thinking that moves beyond this stage to embrace living realities once more. Through this, we can fill Chalcedon's paradoxical abstractions with life.

12

Steiner also brought a vast array of research results that cast light on the Incarnation. They show the same movement that can be seen in the thoughts of the early church fathers. He spoke about the journey of the man Jesus, including the years about which the Gospels are silent. A wealth of detail allows us to understand the experiences and inner transformations that enabled this human being to receive the Word into himself. Steiner also casts light on the long 'descent' of the divine Logos towards the moment of Incarnation, which he describes as the middle-point of the earth's evolution.

Rudolf Steiner's insights into the nature of the human being can be a great help in imagining how the Incarnation worked. One central question was already touched on by Apollinaris, Bishop of Laodicea (died 390). For him, if the divine Logos really descended to the earth and became human, something must have made space for him: he must have displaced the centre of initiative and will in that human being. However appealing this picture may be in its simplicity, it flies in the face of the idea that Jesus Christ was truly human. Steiner often used a shorthand description of the Baptism of Jesus which suggests that he agreed with Apollinaris' picture. However, we shall see how Steiner himself referred to this picture as a simplification. Steiner's insights about Jesus' journey to Baptism allow us to see in him a full human nature, including an I, which is able to unite with the Logos in a unique way.

The Logos

Jesus was born into a dual heritage. His bodily descent is traced in the Old Testament. His other heritage was a world of thought which is summed up in the word Logos. This Greek word is normally translated as 'word', though it has a wider radius of meaning, including thought, principle and logic. We know it from the Prologue of the Gospel of St John: 'In the beginning was the Word – the Logos'. In Genesis, creation takes place through God speaking: successive words bring the kingdoms of nature into being. Ancient mystery wisdom echoed this insight: creation was an outpouring of God's word. The divine Word still resounded through creation. Man's capacity for speech connected him to this divine creativity. In the centuries before Christ, a philosophy of the Logos, rooted in these insights, had been worked out, particularly by the philosophers called the Stoics.

These Greek philosophers saw three moments in the Logos' working: first, there were God's thoughts before creation: the unspoken Word. The purposes and visions of the world already lived within God, the divine poet, before the song of creation began. Then there was the creative, creating Word – 'and God spoke, and there was'. The third moment was the seed-Word or *spermatikos Logos*. For the Stoics, this was the power of becoming in all things; for the Christian philosopher, Justin (*c.* AD 100–165), the seed-Word was at the root of the power of reason within human beings, which comes to life when they think and speak. Salvation is needed because the knowledge of God has been dimmed; the seed-Word implanted naturally in human beings is not enough to bring them back to recognition of the Father. For Justin, the divine being in Jesus Christ was God's Word come to earth to renew the seed-Word within us. To do this, he had to appear in human form. When we apprehend the reality of the Word made flesh, the seed-Word within us is brought back to life and we are restored.

This is the basis of a truly catholic (universal) vision of Christ. Justin speaks of 'Christians before Christ', who used the gift of the Logos to apprehend the reality of God. The universal human activities of thinking and speaking bring the Logos-seed to life within us. This seed comes from the same source as the creative Word. When we perceive and understand the world around us, we are using the same power that created the world. The word within us resonates with the great poem of creation.

Many of the subjects we study end in 'logy', which comes from the same root as *logos*. As well as word, logos means the thoughts that belong to a thing. Our Logos-endowed thinking can uncover the work of the Logos in specific areas: in biology we enlist the power of the Logos to understand life, and in geology to understand the earth. Theology is the study of God, and Christology is the subject where we attempt to grasp Christ, through whom the Logos works. We could equally well speak of logos-ology. When the power of thinking is used to reflect on its own source, we are turning the power of the Logos within us to the Logos himself.

Authority

In the Gospels, people often remark on Jesus' 'authority' – in Greek, *exousia*. Alongside its common meaning, this is also the name of a rank of spiritual beings, who are the creator-beings responsible for the creation of the earth. They are a vehicle for the working of the creative Word himself. Authority is the power to 'author' things, to be the originator of something. We develop true authority when we are aligned with our I, the gift of the World-Authors. This means aligning with the seed word within us.

To speak with authority in the Jewish culture of Jesus' time meant to cite a list of previous authorities. It was hard for Jesus' listeners to understand that he did not quote other 'authorities', but spoke on his own authority. Those who hear Jesus witness the immediacy of Logos-power within him, and they cannot explain it. Even his disciples have to tread a long path before they can recognise it. Only at the very end of his ministry, do they say, 'Now we know that you know all things, and need none to question you; by this we believe that you came from God' (John 16:29f).

The problem of recognising authority has not diminished over time. It remains a challenge and a threat when someone speaks on their own authority, as we see from the destinies of those who have something truly original to say. We also like to compare what someone is saying with what we have heard before. It can be frightening when we meet something new and have no other test than our own inner authority.

In his philosophical works, Rudolf Steiner encourages us to experience our own process of knowing as a path to discovering our own authority. When we reflect on our thinking, we have created the thing we are knowing, and thus we are knower and known at the same time. This gives us confidence in our ability to know, which we can extend to other things we want to know. Such clarity about our own *inner* authority liberates us from needing any outside authority.

Although Steiner's early philosophical works do not mention Christ, we can see them as the human side of 'logos-ology'. We bring the seed word to life when we think. Reflection on the activity of the Word within us builds the bridge between our interior world and the world of spiritual reality.

Since the fourth century, the church has taught that reality is divided into things we know with our senses and things we have to believe on external authority – dogmas. More recently, as part of its journey towards emancipation, the human spirit has rejected dogma along with every outer authority. This has led to a rejection of the idea that there could be a world of spiritual being. Only an experience of our own authority – of the creative power of the Word within us – could give the foundation for human beings to accept such an idea once more.

The sections of this book headed 'Contemplation' are intended to help with this. They are based on Rudolf Steiner's instructions for the inner path. They show a few of the many possible ways of bringing the thoughts presented in the book alive. Rudolf Steiner's book, *Knowledge of the Higher Worlds* gives an overview of Steiner's instructions. In relation specifically to contemplative inquiry, Arthur Zajonc's book, *Meditation as Contemplative Enquiry*, is highly recommended.

→ *Contemplation on the Word* ←

The purpose of this contemplation is to introduce a way of working where we prepare a space in our soul in which a word or phrase can resound, using the sentence, 'In the beginning was the Word.'

We think of the world in all its multiplicity and

---

complexity – the aeons of time, the worlds of space that we witness when we look into the starry sky – and we imagine that all of this was brought forth through the Word that resounds through the ages and continues to resound today.

We imagine hearing this creative word as a song or a chorale sung by a mighty choir of angels. In *The Magician's Nephew,* C.S. Lewis portrays the lion, Aslan, pacing over an empty world singing a song so deep and so high that it embraces the deepest chasms and caves of the earth and the highest stars in the sky. In the imprint of every step he takes, a new creature comes to birth.

We might think of the beauty of creation in nature and its abundance, for example in a rain forest. We imagine that all of the seemingly endless possibilities of creation existed in God as his thought before creation, and came into being through his Word.

As a next step, we turn to our capacity to think and speak. Here, we can call on memories: hearing the first words of a child; our joy when we think something through to the end; reading a piece of poetry where sound and meaning are united in perfect synthesis.

We allow all of this to come alive in our soul. Then we let it fade away, leaving silence. We attend to the silence left once the activity of remembering and imagining has faded away.

In the silence we hear the words, 'In the beginning was the Word,' not thinking about them but allowing them to resound in our soul. Speaking them out loud can be a help. After a while, if the words start to lose intensity, we can speak them out loud, or hear them within once again.

If we can maintain concentration for a minute or two, we might experience that the words come alive in a different way than when we first read them. Then we consciously leave the contemplative space and return to our normal consciousness.

2. Two Worlds?

Our experience of the world is divided. Spirit and matter, feelings and facts, moral law and natural law – these are only some of the divisions that we experience. At the heart of Christianity is the experience that the Incarnation of Christ builds a bridge between the worlds. Is the divide between the two worlds real, or does it only exist in our experience? Understanding the origin of the two worlds and the reason for their division can help us to understand the one who bridges the worlds.

Immortal diamond

In his poem, *That Nature is a Heraclitean Fire and of the Comfort of the Resurrection*, Gerard Manley Hopkins (1844–89) describes his experience of mortality in the face of the vastness of natural forces – the Heraclitian fire. Heraclitus, who lived *c.* 535 – *c.* 475 BC, is remembered today for having said 'all is flux'. For him, what truly *is*, is what is in motion, what is becoming. Hopkins looks at the immense forces of nature – the power of the sun to lift up huge cells of water vapour into the air where they become clouds, the beating of the rain and the restless wind – and he sees human achievements – man's 'firedint, his mark on mind' – obliterated. Then he realises that the mighty forces of nature are also transitory. If such transitory forces so easily obliterate what we achieve, do we have any significance that will not be crushed by the march of time?

Then the images of nature give way to an experience that many people are familiar with – an inner shipwreck, a time of 'foundering'. We join the poet in an initiation in life, where we sense that he is approaching the threshold to a new kind of reality.

Man, how fast his firedint, | his mark on mind, is gone!
    Both are in an unfathomable, | all is in an enormous
dark
    Drowned. O pity and indig | nation! Manshape, that
shone
    Sheer off, disseveral, a star, | death blots black out;
nor mark
    Is any of him at all so stark
    But vastness blurs and time | beats level. Enough! the
Resurrection,
    A heart's-clarion! Away grief's gasping, | joyless days,
dejection.
    Across my foundering deck shone
    A beacon, an eternal beam. | Flesh fade, and mortal
trash
    Fall to the residuary worm; | world's wildfire, leave
but ash:
    In a flash, at a trumpet crash,
    I am all at once what Christ is, | since he was what I
am, and
    This Jack, joke, poor potsherd, | patch, matchwood,
immortal diamond,
    Is immortal diamond.

Gerard Manley Hopkins

Reading about this shipwreck, we might be reminded of Jonah,
the unwilling prophet in the Old Testament. Jonah hears a call to
go and prophesy to the people of Nineveh, and he does not want to
do it. So he decides to run away by taking a passage on a ship bound
in the opposite direction. When it is caught in a terrible storm, he
realises that he has brought this fate on himself and his shipmates,
and he confesses to them. They throw him overboard, and he
sinks down beneath the waves, to the 'roots of the mountains'.
He is trapped in seaweed, certain to drown. Suddenly there is a
turning point, and he starts to speak of how he will praise God.
Mysteriously, finding the power to call out the name of God gives
him the strength to come up from the pit and resume his task.

19

As Hopkins sinks into despair, he finds the strength within himself to cry 'enough – the Resurrection!' The call itself seems to release the power of resurrection within him. He finds himself changed into 'what Christ is' through the reality of the Incarnation. Logos-power stirs within him when he finds the courage to proclaim the Logos.

Like Hopkins, we can experience ourselves as 'Jack, joke, poor potsherd, patch, matchwood'. This is the experience of transitory being, the trash and ashes that will be swept away in the tempest, leaving nothing at all. We fear this experience and flee from it. Many of us bear an accumulation of negative images of ourselves that we have taken in and which we fear live in those around us – that we are laughable and ridiculous, shameful and ultimately unlovable. In becoming 'what I am' – in assuming humanity, with all its limitations – Christ makes it possible that I may become immortal diamond. Isaiah's prophecy of the Suffering Servant shows that healing can only come from one who knows the reality of the the poor potsherds:

> He had no beauty or majesty to attract us to him, nothing
> in his appearance that we should desire him. He was
> despised and rejected by mankind, a man of suffering, and
> familiar with pain. Like one from whom people hide their
> faces he was despised, and we held him in low esteem.
> Surely he took up our pain and bore our suffering, yet we
> considered him punished by God, stricken by him, and
> afflicted. But he was pierced for our transgressions, he was
> crushed for our iniquities; the punishment that brought
> us peace was on him, and by his wounds we are healed.
> (Isa.53:2–5).

The Messiah – the messenger from the world of glory – appears in the guise of patch and matchwood to bring us healing. Two worlds need to be joined – but where does the division come from?

The circulation of glory

A poet gave us the words to articulate our question. A seer gives the insight we need to start to answer it. Apocalypse means the unveiling of the inner side of reality. The Book of Revelation is called Apocalypse in Greek. At the beginning of the Book of Revelation, John's vision of what underlies all being is recorded:

> There before me was a throne in heaven with someone sitting on it. And the one who sat there had the appearance of jasper and ruby. A rainbow that shone like an emerald encircled the throne. Surrounding the throne were twenty-four other thrones, and seated on them were twenty-four elders. They were dressed in white and had crowns of gold on their heads. From the throne came flashes of lightning, rumblings and peals of thunder. In front of the throne, seven lamps were blazing. These are the seven spirits of God. Also in front of the throne there was what looked like a sea of glass, clear as crystal. In the centre, around the throne, were four living creatures, and they were covered with eyes, in front and in back. The first living creature was like a lion, the second was like an ox, the third had a face like a man, the fourth was like a flying eagle. Each of the four living creatures had six wings and was covered with eyes all around, even under its wings. Day and night they never stop saying: 'Holy, holy, holy is the Lord God Almighty, who was, and is, and is to come.'
>
> Whenever the living creatures give glory, honour and thanks to him who sits on the throne and who lives for ever and ever, the twenty-four elders fall down before him who sits on the throne and worship him who lives for ever and ever. They lay their crowns before the throne and say: 'You are worthy, our Lord and God, to receive glory and honour and power, for you created all things, and by your will they were created and have their being.'
> (Rev.4:2–11)

This vision transports us to a time before time. The great movement that proceeds from the throne and comes back to the throne in the form of the praise of the various beings is a never-ending, self-contained, perfect cycle. The sea of glass encloses what goes on.

How can we understand 'giving glory'? It might be helpful for a moment to recall experiences of glory: the glory of a child taking his or her first steps; the glory of the Alps at sunrise, or of the Milky Way; the glory of a Beethoven symphony or of a Shakespeare play; the glory of work well done; the glory of truly meeting each other in community. All of these experiences and many more can fill this word with meaning. Our experiences are a pathway to the reality of glory. Glory – in Greek *doxa* – is the shining revelation of the inner being of the divine. In the Book of Revelation, this glory is a substance, which circulates around the throne, radiating out and returning in an eternal cycle. The four living creatures and the twenty-four elders receive glory and return it to the throne from their deepest being. They experience glory, recognise it and confess it in one action. Their knowledge of glory becomes a confession from their deepest being, which allows the stream of glory to be returned.

A new beginning

Then I saw in the right hand of him who sat on the throne a scroll with writing on both sides and sealed with seven seals. And I saw a mighty angel proclaiming in a loud voice, 'Who is worthy to break the seals and open the scroll?' But no one in heaven or on earth or under the earth could open the scroll or even look inside it. I wept and wept because no one was found who was worthy to open the scroll or look inside. Then one of the elders said to me, 'Do not weep! See, the Lion of the tribe of Judah, the Root of David, has triumphed. He is able to open the scroll and its seven seals.' Then I saw a Lamb, looking as if it had been slain, standing at the centre of the throne,

encircled by the four living creatures and the elders. The
Lamb had seven horns and seven eyes, which are the seven
spirits of God sent out into all the earth. He went and
took the scroll from the right hand of him who sat on the
throne. And when he had taken it, the four living creatures
and the twenty-four elders fell down before the Lamb.
Each one had a harp and they were holding golden bowls
full of incense, which are the prayers of God's people. And
they sang a new song, saying: 'You are worthy to take the
scroll and to open its seals, because you were slain, and
with your blood you purchased for God persons from
every tribe and language and people and nation. You have
made them to be a kingdom and priests to serve our God,
and they will reign on the earth.' (Rev.5:1–10)

The transition to this chapter can feel like a shock. The elders
and the living creatures face a limit to their capacities. They cannot
open the scroll; they cannot even look at it. In the last chapter, it
would have been unthinkable that there was something that could
not happen. Everything that could happen, was happening. There
was only 'yes'. Now there is 'no'.

And what is this thing which is 'not', which is 'no', which the
heavenly beings cannot even look at? A scroll or a book may tell
a story, with a beginning, a middle and an end. Whatever moved
in Chapter 4 returned to itself. There was no story, but an endless
circulation. God was all in all. In this world of perfect knowledge
and uninterrupted glory, there could never be a story, a drama
with an uncertain outcome. Yet only through that being possible
can there be freedom, and the free choice of creatures to love each
other and love the world of their origins.

Another shocking image is the Lamb who seems to have been
slain, who is the only one capable of opening the book. Something
of the original perfection, unity and clarity has had to die so that
the story can begin and evolution can unfold.

Origen

The Greek Christian theologian Origen (184/5–253/4) created the first systematic theology, which means an explanation of the world through the eyes of faith. In his picture of the beginning of the world, rational beings or *logikoi* were created in the image of the divine Word, or Logos. They were created perfect and equal. God, who has no differentiation within himself, could not possibly create 'better' or 'worse' creatures. However, the *logikoi* were capable of change and development. They were endowed with free will.

In addition to being created in the image of the Word, these creatures have the potential to bring the power of the Logos to life within themselves – hence their name, *logikoi*. All creatures are on a journey from the 'image' of God, the original endowment of their being, towards the 'likeness' of God. This is the journey from creature to co-creator. Creatures are destined ultimately to add to the glory of the beginning. To begin with, however, they remain next to God and behold him, filled with the fire of his glory. Origen describes the beginning of their path of development in strongly anthropological, moralistic terms:

> ... slothfulness, and a dislike of labour in preserving what is good, and an aversion to and a neglect of better things, furnished the beginning of a departure from goodness ... According to its actions, each rational being, neglecting goodness either to a greater or more limited extent, was dragged into the opposite of good, which undoubtedly is evil. From which it appears that the Creator of all things admitted certain seeds and causes of variety and diversity, that He might create variety and diversity in proportion to the diversity of understandings, i.e., of rational creatures. *(On First Principles,* II 9:2).

The fall of the *logikoi* brings about a world which is separate from God, separate from the circulation of glory. Depending upon how much the original fire cools within them, the creatures fall more or less far. This is the origin of the variety of beings in the world. The Seraphim hardly fall away from God at all; the demons have fallen very far indeed. As they distance themselves from God, they lose their clear knowledge of him. This is the cosmic origin of sin, the state of being separate from our origin.

Origen does not explain how he arrives at his account of the beginning of the world. Although it is far less elaborate than the Gnostic theories of the beginnings of the world, with their detailed accounts of the creation of successive ranks of spiritual beings, it seems like them to have emerged not from logical thought but from mystical contemplation. As in the great Gnostic systems, the material world emerges in stages from the spiritual world, which is its origin and remains its inner being. The fire of God's glory smolders within the world of the senses.

By the fourth century, mystical intuition was no longer acceptable as the foundation for thinking about the world. The Church had to safeguard the reality of the spirit through dogma. Experiences in the world and the truths of heaven became ever more separate.

Esoteric science

We have seen that our experience encompasses both transcendent glory and the reality of the sense-world. If we are to do justice to both of these kinds of experience, we need to find a method that can encompass them both. In his early work, Rudolf Steiner outlined such a method. In his later works, he shared the results of his investigations into reality using this method. If we use these results as meditative pictures, they can stimulate the faculties of our own spiritual perception. Alongside this, we can proceed in a more scientific way and adopt them as hypotheses and see whether they help us to make sense of our experiences.

The background for engaging with the imaginative pictures of the Book of Revelation and making sense of our dual experience of the world comes from Rudolf Steiner's foundational work, *An Outline of Esoteric Science*. The title in translation can bear some explanation. Esoteric comes from the Greek for 'inner'. It has accumulated a certain cultural baggage over the centuries. Steiner makes it clear that for him, esoteric means 'in context'. All our knowing is an attempt to put the fragments that we can grasp in their proper context. In this way, knowing overcomes the sundering from our source that inevitably accompanies our journey to freedom.

In *An Outline of Esoteric Science,* Rudolf Steiner describes the situation of the spiritual investigator. He sees the divided world as one. The sense world is the outer side of a unitary reality. To discover the spiritual within everyday things is apocalyptic – the outside of things falls away. Steiner describes how the journey into the inside of things is also a journey back to their origins. Spirit is the source of all that is. The spiritual world condenses or thickens to become matter. 'By spiritual observation we can trace how the material things, events and entities condense, as it were, out of a previous existence which was spiritual through and through' *(Outline of Esoteric Science,* Ch. 4). What 'condenses' in this way is only a part of spiritual reality – a spiritual world remains as 'the guiding and directing principle.'

One of the deepest questions of theology is how there can be something other than God. How an almighty and all-present being limit himself, so that there can be a world over against him? It seems that only an opposing principle – a negative, adversary power – can lead the world away from God. What we experience in the world that does not reflect God's glory is under the influence of this power.

In his lecture cycle *The Inner Experiences of Evolution,* Rudolf Steiner shows that a sacrifice underlies the differentiation of the beings of the spiritual world. There are nine ranks of angelic hierarchies, normally grouped into three groups of three. Perhaps confusingly, these groups are referred to as the First Hierarchy (Seraphim, Cherubim and Thrones), the Second (Spirits of Wisdom, Spirits of Movement and Spirits of Form) and the Third Hierarchy (Archai, Archangels and Angels). In the course of evolution, which begins for Steiner long before the beginnings of our universe, some beings step out

26

of the forward-moving stream of evolution in order to create the resistance through which growth and forward movement can occur. Steiner describes the moral quality of this sacrifice as 'creative resignation'.

We can use Steiner's description to understand the great pictures of the Book of Revelation. In the glory that circulates in the vision of Chapter 4 of that book we can see a spiritual substance. Rudolf Steiner describes how the world begins when beings of the First Hierarchy give the foundation of existence when the Thrones offer up their own substance to the Cherubim, who receive what is offered.

> The Thrones offer and continue their sacrificial activity;
> so that we have there the sacrificing Thrones and a host
> of Cherubim to whom, as we see, the sacrifice rises, while
> they take into themselves the heat which flows forth from
> it *(Inner Experiences,* Nov 14, 1911).

The unsealing of the seals in Revelation 5 marks the moment when evolution begins through the resistance provided by an opposing principle. Rudolf Steiner gives the background for this. In contrast to those Cherubim who receive the sacrifice and send it all back, 'another host of Cherubim accomplish something else; these renounce the sacrifice, they do not accept what is offered them.' Through this, the circulation is interrupted. The substance that has been refused starts on its own circulation, outside the original one. This results in the following situation: 'we have permanent clouds of sacrifice in space; Sacrifice that ascends, Sacrifice that descends, Sacrifice accepted and Sacrifice rejected ...' *(Inner Experiences,* Nov 14, 1911).

The substance that falls out of the circulation of glory is the field in which independent beings can be at work. They behave in the opposite way to the Cherubim. Where the Cherubim renounced, these beings grasp what was renounced and make it their own. Ultimately, this will prove futile, because there is only one reality. However, it is in line with the purposes of the progressive spirits of creation that this seemingly independent

27

reality should come into being. Freedom can only emerge in a world which is independent from its source.

> To make it possible for beings to become thus
> independent, renunciation previously took place. Thus,
> in cosmic evolution it is the case that the gods themselves
> called their opponents into being. If the gods had not
> renounced the sacrifice, beings would not have been able
> to oppose them. *(Inner Experiences,* Nov 21, 1911).

Dualism

The French philosopher René Descartes (1596–1650) made a distinction between two fundamentally different kinds of things. There are things that think – the mind – and things in space. Mind exists outside of space and follows different laws than those that obtain in the sense-world. Things in space have no mind. This is what is called Cartesian dualism. Reality is twofold. The question whether and how the two parts of being can be joined has plagued philosophers ever since.

When we read words like *maya,* the Sanskrit word for illusion, in Steiner's writings, it is easy to think that he believed that there are two worlds, an apparent one and a real one. But in fact, he shows that the division of the world is itself maya. Maya is the product of the state of mind that chooses to concentrate solely on physical manifestations instead of seeing them as the result of spiritual processes.

We live in one world, but our divided experience is very persistent. We divide the stream of experience into two when it meets us. We perceive a world without conceptual content, and bring concepts to bear on what we perceive. This is what we call knowing.

This way of looking at the world is not an aberration. It is at the root of our capacity to be free. It is connected to the two kinds of being, the glory and the potsherds. What we experience as sense-perceptions without concepts is the result of creation having been cut off from its creator. We experience reality divided into two kinds of being because of the decision of the creator-spirits to renounce. However, there is a grave danger: the secondary reality is always threatening to become separate and independent.

Human consciousness has developed in a way that mirrors this cosmic process. To begin with, thinking meant opening our mind to see the reality of glory – as is expressed in the word 'idea', which comes from the Greek *idein,* to see. Even in the divided world, human beings in ancient times could perceived spiritual beings within and behind the phenomena of the sense world. We shall see later how the Church was largely responsible for outlawing the remnants of this kind of seeing in the fourth and fifth centuries.

On our journey towards free individuality, we close our minds off from the greater reality that would otherwise engulf us. John the Baptist's call of *metanoiete!* (expand your consciousness!) was a call to make thinking cosmic once more.

Knowing Jesus, who is 'the guide on the path to this knowing' (John 1:18) is the beginning of healing in the Gospel of St John. Setting out on the path to knowing him means that we allow his power to come to life in us. This life connects us with ultimate reality – with eternal life: 'Now this is eternal life: that they know you, the only true God, and Jesus Christ, whom you have sent' (John 17:3).

3. Who is the Son of God?

Our experience of the divided world has its roots in the will of divine beings that human beings should dwell in a world in which they develop true freedom. Through the Incarnation, Christ bridged the divide. Once it was clear that this achievement was greater than what any human being could manage, the question remained: who is the divine being whom we encounter in Jesus Christ?

The Council of Nicaea

The Emperor Constantine (c. 272–337) was deeply convinced that the Christians' God had helped him to become the sole Emperor of Rome. He believed that this power would be his divine patron and an instrument for achieving his ends. He showed first toleration and then favour to the Church as no other emperor had before him.

The Council of Nicaea, which took place in 325, marked this huge reversal in the fortunes of the Church. Some of the bishops who had been summoned to the imperial palace as honoured guests had still experienced persecution for being part of an unlawful sect, suspected of undermining the unity of the Roman Empire. Constantine convened the first session of the Council, resplendent in his golden robes. The bishops showed their reverence to him by remaining standing until he had sat down. The Roman Emperor, who was not baptised until his death-bed* had expressed his hope that the Church would act as an instrument of state policy, ensuring the harmony of all the imperial subjects.

* This was a custom in an age which saw no possibility for the remission of sins committed after baptism.

For I was aware that, if I should succeed in establishing, according to my hopes, a common harmony of sentiment among all the servants of God, the general course of affairs would also experience a change corresponding to the pious desires of all. *(Letter to Bishop Alexander,* 1).

Constantine attended some of the sessions of the Council, and he may have been behind the insertion of the key term in the creed that the Council approved. In the letter quoted above, Constantine summarises the dispute which had broken out and was causing dissension in the whole church:

How deep a wound did not my ears only, but my very heart receive when it was reported that divisions existed among yourselves more grievous still ...! You, through whose aid I had hoped to procure a remedy for the errors of others, are in a state which needs healing even more than theirs. And yet, now that I have made a careful enquiry into the origin and foundation of these differences, I have found the cause to be of a truly insignificant character, and quite unworthy of such fierce contention. *(Letter to Bishop Alexander,* 4).

This 'insignificant' dispute concerned the possibility of the two worlds being joined, or in the language of the Creed, the question of how Jesus Christ could be part of our world and part of the divine order at the same time.

Arius (a priest in Alexandria, who lived 256–336) saw God as utterly different from the world. God is all knowing, all-powerful and beyond time, unique, indivisible and utterly self-sufficient. Such a God cannot be involved in the processes of change and growth, of suffering and limitation that our world brings. So the one whom we meet in Jesus Christ cannot be of the same kind of being as God. As the created Word of God, through whom the rest of creation came into being, he is far greater than we are – but he belongs to the order of created things. Origen had perceived a possible bridge between the world of eternity and our world in the image of the Son being 'eternally begotten' by the Father. This picture encapsulates a paradox: birth is an event, and therefore belongs in time; eternity means either no time or endless time. The intellect cannot satisfy itself with a mystical approach to them, which simply allows them to stand; it wants to resolve the paradox. Which is true? Eternal or an event? Arius' thinking could not embrace the mystical reality of this paradox.

It is likely that Arius said 'there was a time when he [the Son] was not'.* Only God is eternal. If Christ is called Son, it is because this greatest of all creatures is rewarded for his obedience to the Father's will by being adopted to sonship. This is not the same concept of adoption that the Ebionites (a Jewish Christian movement) held, who thought that Jesus was merely a man whom God adopted as we might adopt a child. For Arius, the Logos is a mighty spiritual being. Nevertheless, his sonship is not 'natural'. Like an adopted child, he is accepted into a context where he does not naturally belong.

Athanasius (priest and later Bishop of Alexandria, lived 296–373) grasped the fact that the Incarnation of Jesus Christ gives us a new insight into the nature of God himself – in Jesus' words: 'if you know me, you know my Father also'. The Father is and always has been 'Father', begetting the Son, and the Son has always been Son, receiving being from the Father. The Divine Son belongs to an utterly different order of being than ours. He is part of the Holy Trinity.

Although they were bitter opponents, Arius and Athanasius shared a conviction that the two worlds cannot be joined. For Arius, the Logos belongs on this side of a dividing line separating time from eternity. Christ is the first and greatest creature, the being through whom God creates the world. Through his Incarnation as man, this greatest of all creatures could draw human beings closer to their origin in the heavenly world. For Athanasius, the relation between the world and its creator and saviour is miraculous. Creation happened 'out of nothing'. Nothing links this world with the glory of its origins; nothing can

---

* Arius' writings were only preserved by his opponents and may have been partially falsified, so we do not know exactly what he said.

reconnect what was never connected. Salvation is as miraculous as creation was.

The outcome of the Council of Nicaea was a creed. The original version was shorter than the one we know today as the Nicene Creed.* The shorter text is:

> We believe in one God, the Father Almighty, Maker of all things visible and invisible. And in one Lord Jesus Christ, the Son of God, begotten of the Father, Light of Light, very God of very God, begotten, not made, being of one substance with the Father; by whom all things were made; who for us men, and for our salvation, came down and was incarnate and was made man; he suffered, and the third day he rose again, ascended into heaven; from thence he shall come to judge the quick and the dead. And in the Holy Spirit. But those who say: 'There was a time when he was not;' and 'He was not before he was made;' and 'He was made out of nothing,' or 'He is of another substance' or 'essence,' or 'The Son of God is created,' or 'changeable,' or 'alterable' – they are condemned by the holy catholic and apostolic Church.

The decisive term in this creed is 'of one substance with the Father', which in Greek is *homoousion* or 'consubstantial'. This term may have been introduced by Constantine on the advice of his court bishop. It had a history in the Trinitarian controversies of the early church, and was viewed with suspicion by many of the bishops at the Council. In spite of this, it was adopted, and it became the touchstone of Christian orthodoxy.

The root of *homoousion* is the word *ousia,* or substance. Nowadays, we generally use substance to mean the stuff that something is made of. This would give rise to a rather materialistic picture of the Trinity, as if there were a common divine stuff shared out among three individuals. Whilst substance could mean

* The creed that we know as the Nicene Creed was the outcome of the Council of Constantinople in 381, when the debates about Nicaea were finally brought to a close. Technically it should be called the Niceno-Constantinopolitan.

something like this in the ancient world, it could also mean the nature of a thing, or its essence.

What the formula *homoousion* came to mean was that the three persons of the Trinity are not three distinct gods but three divine persons who share the same divine nature. All the speculation about the Trinity that had gone before had stressed either the oneness of God or the threeness. Those stressing the oneness suggested, for example that the persons of the Trinity were merely aspects or modes of expression of God's being, hence their name 'modalists'. (The term *homoousion* itself had been used by modalist theologians; this underlay the suspicion with which it was viewed at the beginning of the Council.) On the other hand, stressing the threeness could degenerate into Tritheism, the doctrine that there is not one God but three.

With the doctrine of consubsantiality, the conceptual framework for thinking about the Trinity was given. However, the emphasis on the one divine nature, which is utterly different from the nature of our world, made the division between the two worlds seem far wider than before. God could now be defined but not experienced. Nothing in our world could reconnect us to our original ground in God. Only the Church could bestow salvation. The theology of Nicaea stands behind destruction of pagan shrines by Christian monks in the 380s. The sacred groves were burned down and the temples destroyed, because no religious practice based on an awareness of the spiritual forces at work in the world could be allowed to stand.

The fullness of the Godhead

In the first chapter of the Letter to the Colossians, St Paul points to the relationship between the incarnate Christ and God, when he says that 'he is the image of the invisible God'. This 'invisible God' is the uncreated Word that Athanasius perceived. Paul goes on to point to the beginning of this exalted being, the created Word, who is the 'firstborn of all creation'. We learn that this being is the creative principle that underlies the world. The fullness of the heavenly beings dwells in him (Col.1:15–19).

Experience of the *pleroma,* the fullness of spiritual beings who animate and ensoul every created being, was part of everyday experience in the ancient world. The world was dense with 'gods'. They appeared again in the great medieval systems of the ranks of angelic hierarchies. However, there was a difference. In a world created from nothing by divine decree, the angelic beings were placed outside creation in the timeless, unchanging world of God. The angels were absorbed in the beatific vision of God in heaven. They beckoned human beings to join them there for their salvation. The only angel that underwent a development was Lucifer, whose fall from grace was the beginning of all the troubles that afflict us. To fall away from the original perfection could only mean catastrophe.

Rudolf Steiner brought new insights into the work of beings of the spiritual hierarchies, which make it possible to see how they bridge between the two worlds.

> Everything which happens in the material world is only
> the expression of spiritual facts, each thing which we
> encounter in the material world is only the outer sheath of
> spiritual beings (*Spiritual Hierarchies,* April 12, 1909).

The angelic beings are involved in the work of creation, through which they undergo their own development.

Arius sometimes speaks of the Logos having a beginning; sometimes, he says that he existed before time, or as the beginning of time. Rudolf Steiner gives concrete indications that can help us to understand this unclarity. Some of the angelic beings existed before our universe came into being; they had a past in a previous universe in which they had advanced to the level of creator spirits. Others come into being a part of creation. Time itself comes about through the creation of those beings who are called the Beginnings or Archai.

What Arius perceived as the created Word is the totality of the spiritual hierarchies. The Seraphim receive the purposes of the universe. The Cherubim imagine how the world that works to these purposes might come about. The Thrones offer their own substance as the basis of the world. The Kyriotetes or Spirits of Wisdom receive the divine plans worked on by the First Hierarchy and pour them into the forms and gestures of creation. The Dynameis or Spirits of Movement are behind all that comes into being and grows and decays. The Exousiai or Spirits of Form create the container for all this life and development and wisdom. The Archai, Archangels and Angels – are at work in human destinies and history. All of these beings are part of one being, a symphony, a world-system. This organism is the counterpart of the divine Logos, the creative Word of the Father, through whom divine being passes over into the principle of becoming.

The divine Son works through the creative Word in Creation. As he draws closer to the earth he passes through the ranks of the hierarchies successively until he becomes man.

4. Thinking the Incarnation

The attempts to understand the one who bridged the divided world unfolded between the extremes that he bridged: the divine and human worlds. During the first five centuries, the swing from one extreme position to the other grew steadily less, until it became possible to describe the field where the two extremes meet.

Early extremes

We have seen above the extreme represented by those who saw in Jesus a special man, one uniquely dedicated to God's purposes. He had earned the title 'Son of God', through his obedience to God. But he was human and mortal just as we are. The popular idea of the Messiah was that he would be a human being, the king who would free Israel from the Roman yoke. Phrases from the Bible that we hear with Christian ears sounded quite different to those who longed for this human liberator. When Jesus is referred to as the Son of David, this made Jewish listeners think immediately of a new king, in the line of David. Even the title 'Son of God' had a different meaning. When a king was crowned in the ancient Near East, his coronation was seen as his adoption as a son by the god of the people, the folk-spirit. Roman Emperors also referred to themselves as sons of God.

Later, those who saw Jesus Christ as a man were called Ebionites, the poor ones. They were mainly to be found in the Holy Land, and after the destruction of the Temple in Jerusalem in AD 70, they faded from the scene, as the Holy Land stopped being a centre of Church life.

On the other hand, there were Christian thinkers from the

Hellenistic world, inheritors of the philosophical heritage of Plato. For such people it was inconceivable, ridiculous even, to say that God could truly become man. In Greek philosophical thought, God and the world were so utterly different that this statement was simply incoherent. To have an inkling of the absurdity, we might imagine someone telling us: 'Freedom has become a swimming pool!' The two things simply don't belong in one sentence. For such thinkers there could only be one solution: God can only *seem* to have become human. He clad himself in the appearance of humanity, but he could at any time have cast off the disguise. The idea of God dying on the cross was ludicrous. This earned such thinkers the name 'docetists', from the Greek word to appear or seem.

The Ebionites saw the man in the god-man; the docetists saw the god. The need to move beyond these extremes was the stimulus that gave rise to reflection on Christology. As our contemporary author John McQuarrie writes:

> Both ... docetics and Ebionites ... were considered heretical, for if one subscribed to their views, then Christianity *as a religion* became impossible. Jesus could only be Son, Word, Mediator, High Priest and so on if somehow he bridged the gap between God and the human race, and that seems to demand that somehow he must belong to both sides. *(Jesus Christ in Modern Thought*, p. 153).

Origen

For Origen, the paradox at the heart of the Incarnation is a source of wonder:

> But of all the marvellous and mighty acts related of [God], this altogether surpasses human admiration, and is beyond the power of mortal frailness to understand or feel, how that mighty power of divine majesty, that very Word of the Father, and that very wisdom of God, in which were

created all things, visible and invisible, can be believed to have existed within the limits of that man who appeared in Judea. *(On First Principles,* II 6:2)

Origen does not try to resolve the paradox through logical argument. He brings mythological pictures from the same source as his vision of the Creation of the world. He summarises the fall of the *logikoi,* the rational souls, which fell in varying degrees according to their devotion to God. One soul remained, however:

that soul regarding which Jesus said, No one shall take my life* from me, inhering, from the beginning of the creation, and afterwards, inseparably and indissolubly in Him, as being the Wisdom and Word of God, and the Truth and the true Light, and receiving Him wholly, and passing into His light and splendour, was made with Him in a pre-eminent degree one spirit... This substance of a soul, then, being intermediate between God and the flesh ... the God-man is born, as we have said, that substance being the intermediary to whose nature it was not contrary to assume a body. *(On First Principles* II 6:3).

This soul united with Christ so fully that it would have been impossible to distinguish between them:

the metal iron is capable of cold and heat. If, then, a mass of iron be kept constantly in the fire, receiving the heat through all its pores and veins, and the fire being continuous and the iron never removed from it, it becomes wholly converted into the latter; could we at all say of this, which is by nature a mass of iron, that when placed in the fire, and incessantly burning, it was at any time capable of admitting cold? On the contrary, because it is more consistent with truth, do we not rather say ... that it has become wholly fire, seeing nothing but fire is visible in it? And if any one were to attempt to touch or handle it, he

---

* In Greek *psyche,* which means life and soul.

would experience the action not of iron, but of fire. In this way, then, that soul which, like an iron in the fire, has been perpetually placed in the Word, and perpetually in the Wisdom, and perpetually in God, is God in all that it does, feels, and understands, and therefore can be called neither convertible nor mutable, inasmuch as, being incessantly heated, it possessed immutability from its union with the Word of God. *(On First Principles* II 6:5f)

Origen does not tell us the source of his mythological pictures of the creation of the world and the one soul that did not fall. As we have seen, thinking that borrows from such sources is no longer possible by the fourth century.

After Nicaea

The Council of Nicaea came to the insight that the Logos, the divine being who incarnated as Jesus Christ, was of the same nature as the Father. This made the challenge of imagining the Incarnation all the greater. Throughout the fourth century and into the fifth, theologians grappled with this challenge.

Two tendencies in conceiving the Incarnation became apparent. They echoed the earlier extremes, which had now been transposed within the God-man. One tendency was strongly represented in Alexandria, the great melting pot of the ancient world where all the spiritual streams of antiquity came together. Gnostic Christianity grew up there; the great Christian teachers of Alexandria, Clement and Origen, both saw themselves as teaching a true gnosis or knowledge of the Christian mysteries. Their picture of the human being was influenced by the ideas of Plato. The soul comes from a different world and is a stranger in the body, which it animates.

The emphasis in what is sometimes called the School of Alexandria was on the unchanging reality of the divine Logos, who took up dwelling in the carapace or 'flesh' of a human nature.

This picture is sometimes called Christology 'from above' or descending Christology, because it emphasised the descent of the divine Logos into earthly incarnation.

Athanasius is one of the greatest representatives of this school. He sees in the Incarnation the conquest of the human nature of Jesus by the divine nature, like a king entering a conquered city. The divine Word is unchanged by his incarnation, but the human nature has to suffer invasion. 'He became flesh, not that he has been changed into flesh but that he has taken living flesh on our behalf and has become man' (*Ep ad. Epict.,* 8, quoted in Kelly, p. 285).

The thinkers around Antioch had a different heritage. Antioch was closer to the Holy Land in spirit and was the home of some of the great schools of Jewish learning. Theologians in this school paid greater attention to the texts of the Bible and their literal sense, and emphasised the historical reality of the Incarnation, and of the man Jesus Christ. The human experiences and deeds of Jesus Christ are important for our salvation. This is Christology 'from below', or ascending Christology.

The Word and his flesh

Apollinaris (died 380), Bishop of Laodicea, was a fervent opponent of Arianism, which continued to be a force until the 380s. His vision of the divine nature of the Logos was unwavering. He was the first to grasp that the consubstantiality of the Son with the Father must be mirrored by his consubstantiality with us in the Incarnation.

> The supreme point in our salvation is the incarnation of
> the Word. We believe therefore that with no change in his
> Godhead, the incarnation of the Word took place for the
> renewal of man. (Fragment 81, in Frend, p. 95).

The union of the human and the divine must have been more than just an association. This was something that teachers

41

in the Antiochene school were often accused of: if there was an independent human will and mind in Jesus, how far were the two really one, and how far was it merely a collaboration of two separate natures?

For Apollinaris, if there were a rational soul (Greek: *nous*),* a centre of initiative and will in Jesus, this would inevitably mean that the person of Jesus Christ would be drawn into human sinfulness, as it is our rational soul or mind that is corrupted by the Fall and is responsible for our sinful decisions.

> We confess that the Word of God has not descended
> upon a holy man, a thing which happened in the case
> of the prophets, but that the Word himself has become
> flesh without having assumed a human mind, i.e. a mind
> changeable and enslaved to filthy thoughts, but existing as
> a divine mind immutable and heavenly. (*Ad Iovianum*, I,
> quoted in *Catechism of the Catholic Church*, p. 88).

If we try to make our own pictures of the Incarnation come alive, we may encounter the same problems as Apollinaris: surely there cannot be two distinct selves within the God-man? However obedient that man might be to the divine being, such a collaboration is not the Incarnation. However, if something has to be removed from human nature so that divine nature can enter it, it is no longer a fully human nature. Apollinaris' opponents recognised what he could not: the Word-flesh Christology, taken to an extreme, becomes a refined form of docetism. God has not really become man.

Assuming human nature

Like Apollinaris, Gregory of Nazianzus (c. 329–89) was an opponent of Arianism. He saw that the Word-flesh Christology had gone to an extreme in Apollinaris' thought that he could not support, although Apollinaris had been his teacher. Gregory's saw

* The Greek *nous* was the closest equivalent to our concept of I at the time.

that if the Incarnation is to heal human nature, it must involve the whole human being. He introduces the image the 'assumption' of human nature. This means that Christ needs to take on as his own whatever he is going to heal.

> That which He has not assumed He has not healed; but that which is united to His Godhead is also saved. If only half Adam fell, then that which Christ assumes and saves may be half also; but if the whole of his nature fell, it must be united to the whole nature of Him that was begotten, and so be saved as a whole. Let them not, then, begrudge us our complete salvation, or clothe the Saviour only with bones and nerves and the portraiture of humanity. *(Letter to Cledonus against Apollinaris).*

All of the theologians whom we are studying were priests or bishops who celebrated the mass every day. When Gregory allows the reality of the Incarnation as a healing deed to shine out, he is drawing on this experience. The Logos has 'assumed' the whole of one human nature, and with that, all human nature. Now he turns his attention to Apollinaris' teaching.

> But, says such an one, the Godhead took the place of the human intellect [Greek: *nous*]. How does this touch me? For Godhead joined to flesh alone is not man, nor to soul alone, nor to both apart from intellect, which is the most essential part of man. Keep then the whole man, and mingle Godhead therewith, that you may benefit me in my completeness.

Apollinaris' idea that the divine nature needs to displace the human stems from images of the relationship of spiritual 'bodies' that draw too heavily on the physical world. Gregory refers to a statement of Apollinaris that Jesus Christ 'could not contain two complete natures'. He refutes this:

> Not if you only look at Him in a bodily fashion. For a bushel measure will not hold two bushels, nor will the

43

space of one body hold two or more bodies. But if you will look at what is mental and incorporeal, remember that I in my one personality can contain soul and reason and mind and the Holy Spirit; and before me this world, by which I mean the system of things visible and invisible, contained Father, Son, and Holy Spirit. For such is the nature of intellectual Existences, that they can mingle with one another and with bodies, incorporeally and invisibly.

Gregory points out that it was the *nous,* the rational soul or mind that disobeyed the instruction not to eat of the Tree of Knowledge of Good and Evil.

... that which received the command was that which failed to keep the command, and that which failed to keep it was that also which dared to transgress; and that which transgressed was that which stood most in need of salvation; and that which needed salvation was that which also He took upon Him. Therefore, mind [*nous*] was taken upon Him.

Finally, Gregory shows that the true Incarnation is necessary if there is to be any value in our journey away from God and back to him. Of course, God could have miraculously intervened to change the course of history and undo the effects of the Fall of man. But were he to do that, what need would there have been of the whole of human history?

But if they ... take refuge in the proposition that it is possible for God to save man even apart from mind, why, I suppose that it would be possible for Him to do so also apart from flesh by a mere act of will ... Take away, then, the flesh as well as the mind, that your monstrous folly may be complete.

The questions raised by Apollinaris and Gregory's response go to the heart of the mystery of the Incarnation. For Apollinaris, the essence of the human being is a spiritual kernel which sojourns in the 'flesh', an element foreign to it. There could not be two such kernels in one being, and even if there were, allowing another to be there would prevent the purification of the 'flesh' through the divine Logos. The flesh must be safeguarded from any taint of corruption. Gregory has an intuition of a far more holistic picture of human nature. However it is not clear how Gregory saw the solution to the problem that Apollinaris saw. If the Logos 'assumed' Jesus' mind or his I, what stopped the danger of their being two competing centres of initiative within him?

The Word in partnership

The next great dispute that exercised the minds of the theologians had its roots in the School of Antioch and flared up in reaction to the radical Word-flesh Christology of Apollinaris. Diodore of Tarsus (died *c.* 390) stressed that the divine and the human nature of Jesus Christ had to be seen as utterly independent and not part of any kind of union. Theodore of Mopsuestia *(c.* 350–429), a pupil of Diodore, taught that the Logos 'took not only a body but a complete man, composed of a body and an immortal soul' (*Hom. Cat* 5:19, quoted in Kelly, p. 304). This man was subject to sin and error just as we are, but the Word overshadowed him from conception onward. Because of Jesus' triumph over sin, he is found worthy of being called the Son of God from the time of the Baptism. Theodore saw the union of the two natures as the same in kind, even if greater in degree, than when God indwells an apostle or a saint. He called this is the 'union of good pleasure', or *eudokia.* This is far more than a human whim; nevertheless, the bond of good will between the man and the divine being seemed too flimsy a glue to Theodore's opponents.

The climax of the conflict between the two schools came in the fifth century. The dispute was sparked off by the bishop of Constantinople, Nestorius *(c.* 386–450), who took exception to the title that was becoming popular in worship of the Virgin Mary, *Theotokos* – bearer of a God. He felt that this was in danger of confusing the divine and human natures. He proposed instead that the title *Christotokos* be used – the bearer of the Christ, by which he meant the incarnate Jesus Christ.*

In keeping with Antiochene tradition, Nestorius' overriding concern was to keep the distinction between the divine and the human natures. 'I hold the natures apart, but unite the worship.' The God could not be involved in any change through the Incarnation, even to the extent of suffering. Then, as J.N.D. Kelly points out, Nestorius

> thought it vitally important that Christ should have lived a
> genuinely human life of growth, temptation and suffering;
> if the redemption was to be effected, the second Adam
> must have been a real man. (p. 316).

Two natures came together in Jesus Christ. Nestorius imagined each of the natures remaining intact as they cohered into one person *(prosopon)*. Nestorius' opponent, Cyril of Alexandria accused him of separating the two natures. For Cyril, the union had to be more than psychological. Nestorius preferred the term 'conjunction' for the union of the divine and the human; for him, it served to avoid the danger of mixing or confusing the two natures. It was their distinctness that allowed their joining to have the moral power of *eudokia* or good will. 'The union of God the Word with them [the body and the human soul] is ... voluntary' (quoted in Kelly, p. 316)

Nestorius' opponents distorted his intention with this word, and said that he taught an almost casual union of God and Man. Nestorius on the contrary saw it as the deepest bond, such as unites the three persons of the Trinity. Nevertheless his emphasis on the autonomy and independence of the two natures can leave us with the question: did this man really become God?

---

* Readers who are familiar with Steiner's works may need to get used to the fact that neither the New Testament nor the Church Fathers are as consistent in their use of the names Jesus (for the man) and Christ (for the divine being) as Steiner was.

➴ *Working with the Gospels* ⇜

The aim of this section is to introduce a way of working with passages from the gospel so that they come alive in us, so that we can deepen our experience of Jesus Christ.

The setting for the healings is human and there is a wealth of detail that comes from the reality of the Incarnation. A woman touches Jesus' garment in the crowd, and he knows that a power has passed over to her (Mark 5:25–34). He sees an epileptic boy, and sighs as he realises that the disciples have not yet understood how deeply they will have to change before they can perform such a healing (Luke 9:40–44). He uses spittle and dust to anoint the eyes of a man who was born blind, rather like a mother using spittle to clean her child's grazed skin (John 9:1–7). All of these stories touch us even on first reading, but they can be deepened through contemplation.

First we need to familiarise ourselves with the story. This works best if we to read it, then put the Bible to one side and tell ourselves the story, without opening the Bible to fill in any gaps. Then we read the passage again and notice what we missed out. It is good to repeat this until we can tell ourselves the story with every detail. This does not mean that we need to learn the passage by heart, but that we are completely at home in it.

Once we are at home in the story, we paint the scene before our mind's eye as vividly as we can manage. We might notice that when we first read the passage, we were engaged in a kind of shadow-play, arranging hazy concepts into patterns. As soon as we start trying to make the scene come alive, we discover many questions. What colour were the robes that Jesus wore? Did they all wear sandals? What colour was Mary Magdalene's hair? We might feel daunted by the fact that we do not know the answers to many of these questions, or indeed to any of them. The point, however, is not that we become authorities on biblical archaeology, nor that we consult the accounts of seers who claim to be able to tell us these details; rather, we use the detail as a way of making the scene come alive for ourselves. If we work patiently in this way, the images will correct themselves over time.

The final step is to imagine ourselves as a participant in the scene. It is often good to start by imagining that we are a bystander. What would we tell a friend about what we experienced? Ultimately, though, it is good to place ourselves in the role of one of the main protagonists. If I put myself in the situation of the man lying by the pool of Bethesda in John 5, how do I feel, lying there, when Jesus stands, towering over me, asking me a question that seems so obvious and yet puts me into an inner turmoil: 'Do you have the will that I should heal you?'

Finally, we can try to imagine the scene through Jesus' eyes. It is daunting to imagine ourselves healing someone. However, we learn something even through what we cannot do. We can draw on our experiences, for example with a child or a friend in distress, where we might have felt love and compassion streaming from our eyes. We might remember being in the presence of a parent or friend who looked at us with such love. Can we distill the essence of such experiences and intensify them to the point where we can image the gaze of Jesus as he beheld someone who was sick or paralysed or in the grip of demons? Even if we only imagine a part of the story with such intensity, we may find that the whole story comes alive for us.

Synthesis

The disputes of the fourth and early fifth centuries reached a climax and a preliminary conclusion in the Council of Chalcedon in 451. By then, the affairs of the Church and of the State had become so intertwined that it was hard to distinguish between them. In the modern western world, we would be surprised if a new interpretation of scripture, or a new view on the reality of the Incarnation, shook the state to its foundations. The personal beliefs of the Emperor or his consort, and the persuasive power of the bishops who had the ear of the Emperor or his wife could sway theological arguments one way and another. It is hard to imagine that anything good could emerge from this mixture of idealism and pragmatic power politics, with its sometimes Machiavellian manipulations. The Definition of Chalcedon is the result of a historic compromise that attempts to reconcile two apparently irreconcilable positions.

Although the Definition failed in its intention of uniting the divided church, it has stood as a touchstone of orthodoxy in Christian mainstream thought through the centuries; even the great upheavals of the Reformation did not dislodge it from its throne. Today, it is largely neglected.

The great defender of the Alexandrian tendency in the years leading up to Chalcedon was Cyril, Bishop of Alexandria *(c.* 376–444). He comprehensively outmanoeuvred Nestorius and saw him deposed in 431. He combined formidable political acumen and ruthlessness with a powerful theological mind. Although he died before the Council took place, his influence on it was huge and some phrases from his works found their way into the Definition, much to the outrage of his opponents. His followers in Alexandria, on the other hand, were so outraged by the results of the Council, which they saw as a dilution of Cyril's viewpoint, that they rejected the Definition outright.

The Definition of Chalcedon

The central, Christological part of the Definition of Chalcedon is an explanation of how Jesus Christ can be both God and man. The union of the human and the divine natures joins them into one 'person and subsistence' – in Greek, *prosopon* and *hypostasis.* There are four negations that set limits for our thoughts and imaginations of the Incarnation: the two natures are to be recognised without confusion or change. They are not mingled or merged into one, nor does the one change to make way for the other. On the other hand, they should not be thought so loosely associated that they could drift apart or become independent. The two natures join in the closest union, but if they melded them into one, our picture has gone too far, and we are no longer speaking of two complete natures.

First comes the affirmation of the two natures and their 'perfection' or completeness:

> We teach with one voice that the Son [of God] and our
> Lord Jesus Christ is to be confessed as one and the same
> [Person], that he is perfect in Godhead and perfect in
> manhood, truly God and truly man ...

Then we are introduced to the double consubstantiality. Three clauses highlight the similarity and difference:

> consubstantial [*homoousios*] with the Father as touching
> his Godhead, and consubstantial with us as touching his
> manhood; made in all things like us, sin only excepted;
> begotten of his Father before the worlds according to his
> Godhead; but in these last days for us men and for our
> salvation born [into the world] of the Virgin Mary, the
> Mother of God according to his manhood.

Now we come to the challenge to our thinking, which has to think together the contrary negations:

> This one and the same Jesus Christ, the only-begotten Son
> [of God] must be confessed to be in two natures [*ousia*],
> without confusion, without change, without division,
> without separation, and that without the distinction of
> natures being taken away by such union.

By the time of the Council of Chalcedon, three terms from Greek philosophical thought, whose changing and overlapping meanings had been the cause of much misunderstanding throughout the debate, had acquired more or less generally accepted meanings. *Ousia* meant substance or nature. It is derived from the Greek word for being. *Hypostasis* is derived from the words meaning 'stand' and 'under'; often translated as 'subsistence', it came to mean the particular instance of a nature. *Prosopon* originally meant a mask, of the kind actors wore on stage in the Greek drama. It came to mean the self-manifestation of a being, close to what we call person.

When we speak of human nature, the common uniting factor that makes all human beings human, we are thinking of *ousia*. As human beings, we bear a human form; our lives unfold according to the laws that govern human biography. The upsurge of awareness of human rights in the twentieth century was connected with an awareness of the *ousia* of humanity. Before we know anything about another human being, we feel that the simple fact of their humanity has implications for them and for us.

Nevertheless, if we went to the funeral of someone we loved, and the sermon consisted only of the words: 'He was a human being,' we would be disappointed. Vital though it is to know and acknowledge the humanity within each of us, what interests us more is each individual's biography. For the world of *hypostasis,* the sermon might consist of a statement of the barest biographical facts: born in such and such a year, died so many years later. This tells us the specific details about how this individual instance of humanity came to the world. This would still leave us thirsty for more – what did our friend achieve? What was he like? What was his 'firedint, his mark on mind,' to quote Hopkins? What unique things did do with his life? These questions relate to his person or *prosopon*.

The language of nature, subsistence and person takes us through three archetypal stages: being, becoming and self-revealing. We see these stages in world-evolution and in the development of every human being. Our being, through which we are connected to the Father-God, is the foundation of our existence. Becoming – the realm of the Son-God – brings about our individual existence. The Holy Spirit is at work when we manifest our being.

The profound truth embodied in the Definition of Chalcedon

is that the Incarnation must go beyond the level of conscious assent (union of persons). Two apparently utterly unconnected kinds of thing – divine and human nature – join in one individual. Normally, a *hypostasis* can only be an instance of one nature. The *hypostasis* of Jesus Christ is the place where the two natures meet – in closest union without melding into one, and in complete distinctiveness without flying apart. This *hypostasis* in turn reveals itself through the one person, the Lord Jesus Christ – to quote the final lines of the Definition again:

> the peculiar property of each nature being preserved and
> being united in one Person and subsistence [*hypostasis*],
> not separated or divided into two persons, but one and
> the same Son and only-begotten, God the Word, our Lord
> Jesus Christ.

The Definition of Chalcedon sets limits for our thinking about the Incarnation. If we picture two centres of initiative and will in Jesus, we are not in touch with the reality of the one person of the incarnate Lord; if on the other hand, we think that this is a person who merely has divine qualities, we are failing to grasp the Incarnation of a divine being. It is all too easy to explain things that we read in the gospels by saying to ourselves: of course Jesus could do that, because he was actually God. Then we meet a statement such as 'Why do you call me good? Only God is good!' and we have to pass it by. Or 'only the Father knows ...' On the other hand when we read of Jesus' human qualities, when he is tired or hungry, or angry, if we say to ourselves: that's just the man Jesus, the God would never experience such things, we can wonder whether we have really taken seriously the reality of the Incarnation. If the divine Logos has truly become human, he has limited himself by using a human mind to think with and human words to speak with.

Chalcedon did not bring the debates to an end. In fact it was the cause of one of the first great schisms of the Church, which endures until today. As it represented a middle between two extremes, it is not surprising that parties on either side of the argument experienced it as a compromise that gave too much ground to the other side. Nestorian Christians saw in the Definition confirmation that the Church had been taken over by Apollinarians, dangerously confusing the two natures in the incarnate Lord. Supporters of this view found refuge outside the Roman Empire, in Persia. For centuries they were the main missionaries to the East, and the first Christians in China were Nestorians. On the other hand, the reception of the Definition in Alexandria was anything but friendly for the opposite reason. Bishop Proterius was lynched on his return, as the mob of monks and passionate believers felt that he had betrayed the heritage of the beloved Cyril and allowed for two natures after the union, which for them reeked of Nestorianism. The Coptic Church developed as an alternative to Catholic Christianity, and to this day it describes itself as miaphysite, which is to say it holds to there being a single nature after the union.

Attempts to refine the understanding set out at Chalcedon continued, driven in part by a wish to draw those who would not accept it back into communion. The debates make fascinating reading. However, the purpose of this book is not to give a comprehensive historical overview. The Definition of Chalcedon sketches out the terrain in which a living understanding of the Incarnation can unfold. Our challenge now is to investigate how to develop this thinking.

→ *Contemplation on the Definition of Chalcedon* ←

We need to choose a part of a long text such as the Definition of Chalcedon to concentrate on. We might take this central passage:

perfect in Godhead and perfect in manhood, truly God and truly man ... consubstantial with the Father as touching his Godhead, and consubstantial with us as touching his manhood ... in two natures, without confusion, without change, without division, without separation ... united in one Person and subsistence.

First we need to make sure that we are familiar with the text, and that we have understood all of its terms. After understanding them, we can try to fill them with life. What pictures do we have of the Godhead? What is our picture of human nature?

As a next step, we can observe the composition of the Definition. It moves between the worlds – 'Godhead – manhood ... God – man ... with the Father – with us' and so on. We can repeat these sentences to ourselves, moving between the terms, which we have already filled with meaning.

Finally, we could look at the four negations: 'without confusion, without change, without division, without separation'. The negations serve to keep the concepts distinct. To sense the dynamic that is at work, we can try thinking beyond the boundaries: what happens when we imagine the two natures being separated? What happens if they are merged into one? Reading about the struggles of the early church fathers can be a help with this.

The dynamic of the Incarnation is outlined by the four 'withouts'. We might visualise it something like this (see right).

The arrows show the pull of the extremes; the space between the two circles is the free space that opens up through the mutual negations.

We can use all of this as preparation, allowing the thoughts and pictures to come alive within us. Then we can let them fade away, attending to the space in our soul which is left. In this space we hear the sentences from the Definition.

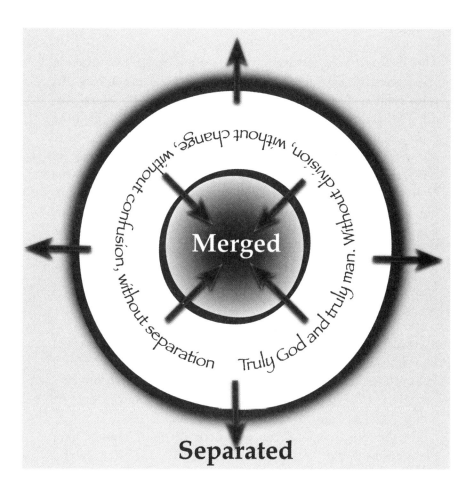

5. A Living Picture

The Definition of Chalcedon opens up a space for thinking the Incarnation in a dynamic field of opposing forces. Its form echoes the reality of the Incarnation, through which two different realities join. The struggles and tensions that filled the centuries before Chalcedon were condensed into the Definition. However, it is cast in the most abstract language. It is easy to sympathise with Schleiermacher's criticism (see p. 12) – the Definition of Chalcedon deals with the most holy of mysteries, but it does not create a feeling of piety. Perhaps we can now feel the challenge contained in the question outlined at the beginning of the book: can we develop a way of thinking that is appropriate for thinking the Incarnation? Can we allow the Logos within us to unfold its activity, so that we can think about the Logos in Jesus?

In *The Philosophy of Spiritual Activity,* Rudolf Steiner invites his readers to go on a journey of reflection on their own process of knowing, and to reflect on the impulses of their actions. This path of knowing, through which true self-awareness and freedom may become possible, is 'logos-ology' through which we can become aware of the seed-Word within us (see p. 14).

At the beginning of the twentieth century, Steiner gave descriptions a path of inner schooling. Through the careful cultivation of all aspects of our soul-life, and through developing the faculties of meditative or contemplative enquiry, the spiritual world can become as real for us as the world that we experience through our earthly senses.

Rudolf Steiner also shared the results of his own spiritual investigations. He made it clear that he did not intend these to be taken dogmatically but as a resource for our own spiritual work.

Allowing these research results to come alive in us helps us to develop the faculties through which Steiner himself arrived at them.

Understandably, those who have found in Steiner a guide on their own inner path have to struggle with the temptation to take his statements dogmatically, as if they were answers that brought inquiry to an end. It is a great help if we have found our own questions before we come to Steiner's insights. Then we can bring his results into dialogue with our own questions and explore whether they help us in our own investigations.

It is also helpful to notice the great array of viewpoints that Steiner brings. He rarely speaks about the same thing from the same point of view twice. His lectures were given on particular occasions to specific audiences and he was not concerned to reconcile every statement he made with all the others that had gone before. Thus his pupils are confronted with a living world of insights, many of which seem at first reading to be contradictory. The academic approach in such a situation would be to decide which statement is 'normative', and relegate the others to a lesser importance. We can also adopt a contemplative approach; then, we need to let each statement live in us in so that a picture emerges that we can see as a living reality, illuminated from many sides. This is what Steiner himself recommends, for example in his Letters to the Members:

> We feel how every thought or picture in which we clothe
> [anthroposophical knowledge] must needs be incomplete.
> We feel that what we bear in our soul is infinitely richer
> than what we can express in thought; and as we grow
> aware of this more clearly, the reverence for the spiritual
> life increases in us. Now this reverence must be present in
> all anthroposophical descriptions. It must be one of the
> fundamental notes. Where such reverence is absent, there
> is no power in the discussion of anthroposophical truths.
> (*Anthroposophical Leading Thoughts,* Letter X).

Tracing the development of the thinking of the early theologians was intended as a way of finding our own questions.

What follows is an outline of a picture of the Incarnation that is made possible through Rudolf Steiner's insights.

Readers are encouraged to pause at this point and take stock of their questions. It could be useful to write down questions in the following areas:

Who is Christ?
Why did Jesus Christ need to be both God and man?
What happened in the Incarnation?

The rest of the book brings many quotations from Rudolf Steiner. Readers will gain the most if they bring these into dialogue with their own questions, and perhaps with the insights of the early theologians as summarised in the Definition of Chalcedon. Then it may be possible to experience how the insights do not bring our own investigation to an end, but allow it to become deeper.

The life of Jesus

Over a number of years I have led seminars in a variety of places on the question 'who was Jesus Christ?' We tried to discover what qualities would need to be embodied by the one called Son of Man and Son of God. I was struck by the way that groups without theological training and in some cases without prior knowledge of Steiner's insights came to the same images. On the one hand, they saw the need for an innocent, virginal human soul, ready to receive the incarnating divine being in devotion and surrender; on the other hand, they imagined a mature soul, full of earthly wisdom, whose efforts made him worthy of union with the divine Logos. These pictures of course echo the different emphases of Christology 'from above' and 'from below' in the fourth century. The question that we then faced was how such different qualities could come together in one human being.

Rudolf Steiner saw that these two aspects of Jesus are reflected in the accounts of Jesus' birth and infancy that are told in the

Gospels of Matthew and Luke. Unfortunately, because there is a rather sensational quality about talking about 'two Jesus-children', the importance of the insights themselves is sometimes lost. Steiner's intention in talking about these truths was not to create a sensation, but to give us detailed pictures of the events of the Incarnation so that we can imagine it more concretely. He sought to remove this essential truth from the realm of dogma and bring it into the realm of clear thought.

Steiner took the gospel accounts very seriously. He points out that the details of the stories are so different that only the names seem to unite them. When we learn that these names – Miriam (Mary is the Greek version), Joseph and Yeshua (or Joshua, again, Jesus is the Greek version) – were among the most common of that time, representing great heroes in the national history of the Jewish people, it becomes less surprising that there could be two families with the same names. The tables of genealogy that are presented in each gospel bear this out. From King David onward, these seem to be two different family trees. The genealogy presented in Matthew (1:1–17) goes from David to Solomon, the greatest king of the united kingdom of Israel. It is a royal line of descent, leading only to the relative obscurity of Joseph because the kingship had passed away from the line of David by the time of Christ. The genealogy of the child described by Luke (3:23–38) passes from David to Nathan, a figure who is only briefly mentioned in the Old Testament. He bears the same name as the prophet who assisted Zadok the priest in the anointing of Solomon and who was the truth-teller to King David. What happens to him after David's death is not described in the Bible.

In the Gospel of St Matthew we hear the story through the eyes of Joseph. He learns from an angel why Mary is with child, and where this child has come from. The child is born at home in Bethlehem, and receives a visit from wise men, or *magi* who have seen his star from far away. These wise men, spiritual leaders of their people, had visited Herod on their search for the child, and Jesus' birth becomes a public event that plays out on the stage of history. Herod plots his infanticide out of fear for his position and

Joseph takes his family into hiding in Egypt, only to return after Herod's death.

The story in the Gospel of Saint Luke takes us into a very different world. There is a prelude with the birth of John the Baptist. The scene is set in Nazareth in Galilee. The angel announces the coming birth to Mary, not Joseph. Mary visits her cousin Elisabeth, mother of John the Baptist, when John leaps in the womb in recognition of the child in Mary's womb. The world of the secrets of motherhood and childhood opens up before our gaze. This is the nativity story that awakens compassion today even in the hearts of those who have never heard the rest of the gospel story: the census, the need for the journey to Bethlehem, where there is no room in the inn, and the birth of the child in a stable. In the greatest contrast to the regal birth that St Matthew describes, the first witnesses to the arrival of this baby are the shepherds who have heard the news from the angelic hosts in the fields.

Most readers of the Gospels read these two stories and harmonise the differences because they 'know' beforehand that they are actually one story. For many scholarly theologians, they belong to the legendary material that grew up around the central message of the gospels, and are not taken seriously as historical accounts. However, the two worlds to which they introduce us resonate with the two qualities that combined in Jesus.

Although we will probably have to acknowledge that we would not have arrived by ourselves at Rudolf Steiner's insight that the different stories actually tell of two different births, his statements about the identity of the souls of the two children resonate with what we have discovered through our own investigations. Steiner's statements rest on the insight that the human soul is not created in the moment of conception, which underpins the dogma of the Incarnation as it is taught today. The essential aspect of the human being is a spiritual kernel which manifests in many incarnations, in a process of gradual learning. Steiner's spiritual anthropology shows a process of 'growing up' – building a basis for existence through developing a physical body imbued with life, within which an interior world of experiences can unfold. This has a counterbalance in a progressive 'growing down' of the spiritual being, which successively inhabits the physical body, life and soul, and then transforms them.

Steiner tells us that the individuality who incarnates as the child described in the Gospel of St Matthew is the same one who incarnated as Zarathustra, the great initiate of the ancient Persian civilisation, who through many lifetimes had worked to establish human culture on the earth. This mighty soul brought a wealth of gifts and experiences with him.

We have seen how Origen taught that the Incarnation was made possible through a pure soul who had remained united with the divine fire. Rudolf Steiner adds a wealth of detail to Origen's picture. Steiner describes how when human beings embarked on their journey of successive incarnations, a human I was 'held back' in the spiritual world. It retained the same qualities as Adam had before his first earthly incarnation. This is the soul who incarnates in the child described in the Gospel of St Luke, who had virginal, almost other-worldly qualities. There are beautiful legends about childhood of Jesus. He takes mud from a stream and blows on it, and a flock of birds flies out of his hands; he walks across the dry fields and grass springs up in his footsteps. These stories probably belong more to the realm of mythical truths; rather than describing historic events, they tell us about the pure forces of life and creativity that surrounded the boy described by Luke, and the pictures that filled the souls of those who met him.

Merging

When we immerse ourselves in the simple, pastoral world of the infancy stories in the Gospel of St Luke, it is all the more surprising when we read about the scene in the Temple when Jesus was twelve (Luke 2:22–40). This simple, docile child disobeys his parents and remains behind when they set off home. They find him in the Temple, continuing what must have been a kind of bar mitzvah, with a great difference: instead of merely answering the questions put him, he puts his own questions to the scholars of the Law. Rudolf Steiner tells us that this marks the moment when the soul of the child whose nativity is described in the Gospel of St Matthew passes over into the other child. In the very moment when he could have entered earthly maturity for the first time, the innocent, unformed soul of the child we read about in the Gospel of St Luke is filled with another.

Puberty is the moment when a child begins to have his or her own independent destiny, separate from the family. Children before puberty cannot really be said to sin, because they have not yet started to develop full self-awareness. The more mature soul enters the child described by St Luke before he has attained this degree of development.

How can we understand this merging of two beings? Gregory of Nazianzus pointed out that spiritual entities can occupy the same space at the same time, unlike physical ones. This insight gave Gregory the key to understanding how the Logos can co-exist with a human mind. Rudolf Steiner's insights show that this co-existing or inhering begins already in the preparation of Jesus for the Incarnation of the divine Logos. The child described by Luke opens himself for another being at the age of twelve. From that age onwards, the centre of the personality of Jesus is the I of Zarathustra, which hitherto had been in relation with the Matthew child, who now fades from the scene. These years, between 12 and 30, are only alluded to briefly in the Gospel of St Luke (2:51f):

> Then he went down to Nazareth with them and was
> obedient to them. But his mother treasured all these things
> in her heart. And Jesus grew in wisdom and stature, and in
> grace before God and men.

Brief though it is, this characterisation points at the two qualities that are now combined in the child: wisdom is the sign of his earthly maturity and the insights brought with him from his vast experience of human life. The stature points to the abundant forces of life that still sustain the child. And in the aspect of grace we can see the result of these qualities combining. The two qualities that are the precondition of the Incarnation have come together.

The hidden years

The gospels are silent on the further destiny of Jesus until he comes to the Jordan for his Baptism. If we read the narrative in St Luke, the change is striking. Something has transformed the self-assured boy, who held his own with the teachers in the Temple, into the one who now humbly submits himself to baptism by John. Rudolf Steiner made a unique contribution to filling out this story with his lectures on *The Fifth Gospel.* These trace the story of Jesus of Nazareth through his formative years of youth and young adulthood, the years in which each of us grows upward towards being able to realise our true being, which happens around the age of 28.

Steiner describes three experiences that Jesus went through as a young man, experiences which led him to feel the grave danger in which humanity found itself. These experiences sum up countless others which Jesus must have had in these years.

From time immemorial, the inspiration for human culture, social life and economic life had flowed from the temples and mystery-centres of humanity. On his journeys through the Holy Land following his father's trade, Jesus sees the desolation of culture that had come about through those spiritual sources running dry. He is moved by the deepest love and compassion for those who are left as it were orphaned.

First, he realises that the *Bath Kohl,* the voice which had inspired the prophets, and whose faint echo had continued to be the spiritual source of the Jewish religion, had grown silent. Then he experiences the dereliction of a heathen temple and its demonic infestation. Finally, he experiences the communities of the Essenes. Here was one group that still cultivated a living spirituality. However, in shutting themselves off from the world, they had given the adversary powers free rein in humanity at large.

These experiences are summarised and distilled in the shocking words of the cosmic or reversed Lord's Prayer, which Jesus hears in the deserted heathen temple.

AUM, Amen!
Evil rules,
Witness of the severing I,
Selfhood's guilt by others owed,
In daily bread now felt,
In which heaven's will be not done,
For man deserted your kingdom,
And forgot your names,
You fathers in the heavens.

This prayer, which comes from the same source as the *Bath Kohl*, characterises the situation of humanity utterly separated from its source in the divine – the 'severing I'. This separation has led not to true freedom but to enslavement to evil – 'evil rules'. The self is the source only of guilt; the web of relationships that connects human beings to each other and to the earth is not the source of community but of debt – 'in daily bread now felt'. The last three lines show the bitter consequence of the trajectory that began with the division of the worlds. The 'severing I' has lost all connection to the world of glory.

In his thirtieth year, just before the Baptism, Jesus has a conversation with his mother in which he pours out his soul and tells her everything that he has experienced. She listens so intensely that he is released. Jesus feels the same urgency about the danger facing humanity and the earth that we normally only feel when we are in personal danger, and his soul leaves his body in the same way that we do when we are in mortal danger. He walks to the Jordan in this state. The greatest of all human souls, inhabiting a body imbued with the freshest and purest forces of life, had to recognise that nothing that he could do would avert the danger. The powers of evil had triumphed, and no merely human forces could halt their progress into the world.

The human destiny of Jesus of Nazareth prepared him to make the journey towards Baptism in a state of complete receptiveness. This human destiny was a kind of recapitulation of all human experience. The two Jesus-children represent two archetypal aspects of human nature and human history. All of the wisdom won from the deeds that founded human culture on earth; all the suffering borne from the experience of the consequences of sin and separation, are contained within the being of Zarathustra. And all that is fresh and young, which retains its connection to the spiritual world in innocence lived in the child that we read about in St Luke. Jesus is a distillation of all the best forces of humanity, uniquely equipped to sense the need in which humanity found itself. In this life that culminates in the journey to the Jordan, we can see an answer to the question posed by those theologians whose focus was on the man, on the vision of Christology from below: what experiences and moral qualities would the human being need, who was to be worthy of union with the Logos?

Baptism

The incarnation of the human I is a process, not a momentary event. This is true of the Incarnation of the Word, as well. Canon A.P. Shepherd makes this very clear in his book, *The Battle for the Spirit* (p. 137):

> The whole process of human rebirth is prepared for and watched over by the pre-earthly human ego, aided by exalted spirit beings, long before the ego itself indwells ... the physical organism. So this whole process of Incarnation is the work of Christ Himself, working out of the spirit-world ...

The Baptism of Jesus in the Jordan is part of a process of incarnation. Shepherd continues:

> In the whole of the mysterious ... process of the Incarnation of Christ described to us by Steiner, beginning with the act of divine initiative, spoken of in the Annunciation, right up to the ... Baptism in the Jordan, we have the single spiritual event of the Incarnation of Christ into the being of Man.

Such a way of understanding the Incarnation is more in tune with our experience than the idea that the Logos was fully incarnated from the moment of conception onwards. Only after reaching maturity do we start to live out of our true being. The life of Jesus has prepared him to unite with the Logos, who now could start to unite with him fully.

> Then Jesus came from Galilee to John at the Jordan, to be baptized by him. John would have prevented him, saying, 'I need to be baptized by you, and do you come to me?' But Jesus answered him, 'Let it be so now; for it is proper for us in this way to fulfil all righteousness.' Then he consented. And when Jesus had been baptized, just as he came up from the water, suddenly the heavens were opened to him and he saw the Spirit of God descending like a dove and alighting on him. And a voice from heaven said, 'This is my Son, the Beloved, with whom I am well pleased.' (Matt.3:13–17).

John (1:32–34) adds the testimony of the Baptist:

> And John testified, 'I saw the Spirit descending from heaven like a dove, and it remained on him. I myself did not know him, but the one who sent me to baptize with water said to me, 'He on whom you see the Spirit descend and remain is the one who baptizes with the Holy Spirit.' And I myself have seen and have testified that this is the Son of God.'

The Holy Spirit is the spirit of connection. At the Baptism, a connection is made between Jesus and the divine Logos, which is not broken. We normally only experience fleeting moments when we feel fully connected with our true being. We can imagine that the many people whom John baptised experienced such a moment of connection with their true being, and that it was this that gave them impulse to change their ways which John preached. When Jesus was baptised, the connection remained.

66

The Baptism is the climax of Jesus' journey. It is also the moment when something quite new irrupts into the world. Rudolf Steiner lived in a time in which the emphasis had been placed on the man Jesus, the 'simple man of Nazareth'. Christology 'from above' was all but lost. In this context, Rudolf Steiner often spoke of the Baptism in a way which sounds very like what Apollinaris taught. In many places he speaks of how the I of Jesus leaves, and the I of the Christ takes its place. He sometimes counts up the members of the being of Jesus Christ: physical, etheric and astral bodies, and instead of the I, the Christ. This simplified picture can free us from an all-too human picture of Jesus, which was the legacy of the liberal Protestantism of the nineteenth century, and which can still be felt in much contemporary theology and popular religion.

Beyond the image of the 'simple man of Nazareth', we are challenged to see in the Incarnation the entry of something quite new into the course of human history.

⇥ *Contemplation on the Baptism* ⇤

The aim of this contemplation is to prepare a space in our soul to experience the reality of the Baptism of Jesus in the Jordan.

Read the descriptions of the life of Jesus from the first part of this chapter. It might be a help to read the lectures of *The Fifth Gospel* to fill out the details. Try to imagine the situation of Jesus; this means that we need to allow what we are reading to have an impact on us, as if it were happening to us. What goes through my soul when I realise the desolation of humanity in the reversed Lord's Prayer? What do I feel when I see that those human beings who have kept themselves pure are unwittingly adding to the effect of the evil?

It could be helpful to draw on memories of times when we felt that we had to give up in the face of a situation where we could see no way forward. Sometimes we realise that we have been struggling even when we thought we had given up. Then comes the moment of surrender, when the pain and loss that we have been resisting become our friends; we let them in, and give ourselves completely to the experience.

This contemplation is based on what has been covered in the book so far, but it would also be good to read the next chapter and return to it. Then we could add the picture of the 'empty sphere' of the I of Jesus, waiting to welcome the divine Word into itself.

If we allow all of this to light up in our soul and then fade away, we could turn to one of the accounts of the Baptism in the gospels and hear it in this listening space. (See Matt.3:13–17, Mark 1:9–11, Luke 3:21f, or John 1:32–34.) If we worked with the gospel reading in the way introduced on page 47, this will add to the intensity of the experience.

The I of Jesus

In *The Fifth Gospel* we learn that Jesus walked to the Baptism in a state similar to sleep-walking. In sleep our awareness of ourselves as an I is interrupted. Our soul and the centre of our personality withdraw. Our will to propel ourselves into life grows still. We are united with our higher self, as we sometimes notice when we awaken from sleep knowing that we have communed with our true being and feeling a renewed connection to our life's deepest purpose.

When Jesus walks to the Baptism, he seems to be without an earthly I; he is utterly open to the promptings of his higher being. Does this mean that he has no I at all? This would mean that Apollinaris had grasped the reality of the Incarnation after all.

We have seen that Rudolf Steiner puts great emphasis on the Baptism as the moment when the divine Logos begins the final phase of its descent into earthly incarnation. We have seen how Steiner's insights allow us to develop far more detailed pictures of that journey than would otherwise be possible. However, he often speaks of the moment of Baptism in terms that recall Apollinaris.

> The fact that the Phantom [the true form of the physical body] could be rescued from death, that depends on the Christ-being being there: physical body, etheric body, astral body ... and no human I, but the Christ being.
> *(From Jesus to Christ,* Oct 11, 1911)

When Steiner is looking more specifically at the reality of the humanity of Jesus, however, he uses more nuanced language:

> It seemed as if this Nathan Jesus-child ... was not in possession of a human I, as if he consisted only of a physical body, etheric body and astral body. And it is quite adequate if we say initially that an I, developed as I's had developed in Atlantean and post-Atlantean times, was not there at all in the Luke Jesus-child. *(From Jesus to Christ,* Oct 12, 1911).

A description which is sufficient 'initially', or 'for the time being' (the German is *zunächst*), is one which we need to develop as our understanding deepens. Steiner draws our attention to what is different about this 'I' – it has not undergone the development that human beings went through in the distant times of prehistory, to which Atlantis refers. This is what we have traced through the story of the two Jesus-children and the renunciation of his opportunity to unfold as self-aware I on the part of the child described by St Luke. As part of his first earthly incarnation, the child described in the Gospel of St Luke would have started the journey towards I-consciousness at the age of twelve. Instead he received the I of the other Jesus child into himself. Before the Baptism, this I withdraws.

We are challenged to imagine how Jesus' I could become the bearer of the divine Logos. Origen brings the image of iron glowing in the fire to express the union of the Logos with the human soul of Jesus. Just as we cannot tell where the iron ends and the fire's glow begins, we cannot see where the divine fire ends and the human bearer of the fire begins.

The *anima candida*, the human soul that remained in closest communion with the Godhead, had not undergone the development that every other human I had undergone. Our experience of ourselves is based on our past. We build our identity from what we have experienced and achieved in this life and in preceding ones. None of this was possible for Jesus. He had accumulated no earthly experiences, and had not been the author of any deeds of his own. He had no earthly personality. Nevertheless, he had a human 'I'. He was 'consubstantial' with us. Rudolf Steiner sometimes distinguishes between two aspects of the I: the I-body or I-bearer, and its content. The one who approaches the Jordan like a sleep-walker is a human being, but he is hardly individual. His I is empty. When the most mature human being of human history had reached the point where he let go in resignation about the future of mankind, he left behind the most innocent human soul, who alone can receive the divine Word into himself.

Rudolf Steiner gives more detail to the picture of the *anima candida* that Origen brought: when human beings started to incarnate on the earth,

> A certain I-substance was not brought into the stream
> of physical incarnations. ... Something was held back:
> an I that was now protected from entering into physical
> incarnations. Instead, this I preserved the form, the
> substance, which man had had before proceeding to his
> first earthly incarnation. *(From Jesus to Christ,* Oct 12,
> 1911).

When Jesus came to be baptised, this I was still in the state that Adam's soul had been in before the Fall. Rudolf Steiner describes this I in some detail.

> ... it was untouched by all Luciferic and Ahrimanic
> influences; it was something which we can imagine in

70

comparison to all other human egos like an empty sphere, in fact only as something that was still utterly unsullied by any earthly experience, a nothing, a negative in regard to all earthly experience. *(From Jesus to Christ,* Oct 12, 1911).

Lucifer and Ahriman are the tendencies which constantly draw us into one or another extreme. Lucifer seeks to draw us away from the earth in fantastical vanity and pride. He claims that his glory is the only glory. He is the spirit of the selfish self, preoccupied entirely with itself. Ahriman seeks to crush us under the weight of earthly necessity in cynical pragmatism. His answer to Lucifer might be to deny that there is any glory at all.

The I has a twofold nature: it is a channel through which the impressions of the world can flow, and it is a centre of initiative and will. Its natural relationship with the world is perfectly harmonious: pure perception would give rise to impulses perfectly reflecting the reality it perceived. The inner life would mirror the world perfectly. The challenges of the adversaries draw us out of this harmonious relationship. What we do when we are out of harmony with ourselves and with the world leaves its traces in our soul.

We can imagine the virginal quality of an ego never touched by these forces. It would be 'like an empty sphere', a vessel that enclosed a middle in perfect balance. The empty sphere is the ultimate space of potential, waiting to be filled. The words 'a nothing, a negative', surely do not mean negative in the normal sense. Rather, this is negative like the negative of a photographic film – the counterpart of experience, a space waiting to be imprinted with experience. This is 'negative capability' – the capacity to allow experience to unfold without own willing or wishing.

This description helps us to understand the biography of the child whom we read about in the Gospel of St Luke. The stages of becoming an earthly I, which all other children go through, had passed him by. Did the axes of his eyes ever meet, as happens soon after birth when a baby starts to look at the world from his or her own perspective? He did not develop an earthly personality, borne down by the weight of earthly being. His ego was, in comparison with every other earthly human being, a 'provisional I' as Steiner called it *(According to Luke*, Sep 18, 1909).

Descent and ascent

The evolution of human consciousness reflects the cosmic drama in which beings separated from the stream of glory and fell away from their origin. The journey leads them towards their self-enclosed, self-aware I. Only by developing such an I can human beings develop the freedom which is the precondition for their fulfilling the mission of the earth: that human beings may learn to love in freedom. However, this journey risks cutting the I loose from any connection with the spiritual world. The movement of the Incarnation implants a new possibility in the human I. The I of Jesus is the place where a new connection with the spiritual world is forged.

The danger of developing self-awareness is that self will become all. In a lecture given in 1922, Rudolf Steiner describes the Incarnation as follows:

> Now there were human beings in the middle of the earth evolution who started to say 'I' to themselves, who raised their I to consciousness within themselves. Into one such human being, which was Jesus of Nazareth, the Son-principle, the Christ-principle now moved in. This Christ-principle thus entered and permeated the I. (*The Mystery of the Trinity*, July 30, 1922).

The phrases 'moved in' and 'entered and permeated' are both attempts to render the German verb *einziehen*, which has two overlapping circles of meaning: on the one hand it means to enter or to move into, as when we move house. On the other hand it means to suffuse or pervade, as when a fragrance fills a room. The empty sphere of Jesus' I is pure openness and potential; the divine Logos enters it, makes it his dwelling, and permeates it through and through with divine substance. All of this fills out the picture of the Incarnation into the empty sphere, the vessel of Jesus' I. The Logos becomes the guiding centre of initiative and will in Jesus. He is the one 'person' who 'subsists in two natures'. If we meditate deeply on the quotation, however, we wonder why Steiner emphasises the I-consciousness before bringing the image of Christ entering and permeating the I. In the dynamic picture of the Incarnation, can we imagine that Jesus does become self aware? Can we imagine that there is an awareness that arises as the potential for awareness is given away?

In a lecture from his cycle on the Gospel of St Luke, Rudolf Steiner speaks about the role of the I of Jesus in making the Incarnation possible.

Only the one I which came to the Earth as the Nathan Jesus and into whose bodily constitution, when this had been duly prepared, the Individuality of Zarathustra passed – this I-being alone could bring to fulfilment within itself the all-embracing Christ-principle. (*According to Luke,* Sep 26, 1909).

This is an image of active cooperation. How can we imagine this, without seeing two distinct centres of initiative and personality in the God-man, as Nestorius seems to have done?

The I is a centre of pure spiritual activity. When we are utterly absorbed in some task that we have set ourselves, we live in the pure activity of the I which connects itself to the world and channels the impulses of our souls – as Steiner says in *Theosophy* (Ch. 6), 'the "I" receives its nature and significance from that with which it is connected.'

The I of Jesus is pure receptivity. It is connected with all that it experiences through the senses on the one hand, and with the divine Logos on the other. Through this purity, it can bring the divine Logos to fruition within itself. Jesus is not aware of himself as a second centre of personality alongside the Logos; he welcomes the Logos and allows the impulses of the Logos to live in him. This is why it is also possible to look at Jesus after the Baptism and say that he has no I. In the language of Chalcedon, Jesus has no *hypostasis* – he is not individualised.

However, without the participation of a human I, the Incarnation would not have been possible. Only this I could bring Christ to fulfilment within itself. The German word translated with 'bring to fulfilment' is *verwirklichen*. This could also be translated with 'realise'. Literally it means 'make real'. When we witness Jesus Christ teaching, praying, comforting and healing people in the gospels, we are witness to human interactions. The Logos can only become real in the earthly world through the participation of Jesus' I.

We can see the Baptism as a kind of initiation. Jesus comes into relation with the divine Logos, who is the bestower of the higher I.

> Jesus was born twice. [At the age of 30] the being of the sun enters him as his second personality ... The sun-influence of the Christ streamed directly onto the I. *(From Beetroot,* March 12, 1924).

↠ *Contemplation on the I of Jesus* ↞

This contemplation draws together three central quotations from Rudolf Steiner's work, which taken together, give the possibility of meditating on the I of Jesus. The aim is to allow the dynamic within and between the different descriptions to resound in the soul. It works well to read the passages that introduced the quotations in the previous pages. Then we can read the quotations one by one, allowing the significance of the words to resound in our soul. It can be a help to draw pictures, either inwardly or on paper, of the movements described. A sample diagram is included below. We can then let the words fade away, and attend to the quiet that is left in the soul. After repeating this for each of the quotations in turn, we could leave a space in which the totality can resound.

74

[the I of Jesus] was something which we can imagine in comparison to all other human egos like an empty sphere, in fact only as something that was still utterly unsullied by any earthly experience, a nothing, a negative in regard to all earthly experience.

Now there were human beings in the middle of the earth evolution who started to say 'I' to themselves, who raised their I to consciousness within themselves. Into one such human being, which was Jesus of Nazareth, the Son-principle, the Christ-principle now moved in. This Christ-principle thus entered and permeated the I.

Only the one I which came to the Earth as the Nathan Jesus and into whose bodily constitution, when this had been duly prepared, the Individuality of Zarathustra passed – this I-being alone could bring to fulfilment within itself the all-embracing Christ-principle.

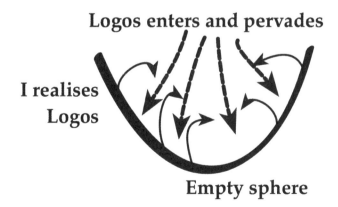

Logos enters and pervades

I realises Logos

Empty sphere

Assuming humanity

Gregory of Nazianzus understood that we are healed through the Logos 'assuming' human nature (see p. 42f). After permeating a human 'I' with his divine fire, the Logos takes on human nature stage by stage through the years until the Crucifixion, which marks the assumption of the physical body. In The Fifth Gospel (Oct 3, 1913), Rudolf Steiner describes this process in the most vivid terms:

> Stage by stage the God became a Man. Like someone who in the throes of unceasing pain becomes aware that the body is steadily declining, so was the Christ Being aware of the waning of His spiritual power while as an etheric Being He was gradually identifying Himself with the earthly body of Jesus of Nazareth ... until the similarity was so complete that He could feel anguish like a man. This is also described in the other Gospel when it is said that Christ Jesus went out with His disciples to the Mount of Olives where He — the Christ Being — had upon His brow the sweat of anguish. Stage by stage the Christ had become Man, had become human, had identified Himself with the body of Jesus of Nazareth.

This healing affects the whole of humanity, not only one human being. There are a variety of images that help us to understand this. The life of Jesus Christ is a 'recapitulation' of humanity's experience since the Fall (compare Eph.1:10). Irenaeus sees this recapitulation in relation to Jesus' experiences of being born and being subject to the conditions of earthly life. By joining us in earthly existence and living a different kind of life, the Logos can set humanity on a new course.

> He has therefore, in His work of recapitulation, summed up all things, both waging war against our enemy, and crushing him who had at the beginning led us away captives in Adam ... the enemy would not have been fairly

vanquished, unless it had been a man [born] of woman
who conquered him ... And therefore does the Lord profess
Himself to be the Son of man, comprising in Himself that
original man out of whom the woman was fashioned, in
order that, as our species went down to death through a
vanquished man, so we may ascend to life again through
a victorious one; and as through a man death received the
palm [of victory] against us, so again by a man we may
receive the palm against death. (Irenaeus, *Against Heresies*,
5:21.1)

The insights from *The Fifth Gospel* fill out this picture. The
children whom we read about in the Gospels of Matthew and
Luke represent two great streams of human history and culture,
which are at the same time the elements of innocence and
experience that are present in every human biography. When
the stream of kingly experience is united with the stream of the
innocent shepherds, all of humanity is present in Jesus. Even
when the I of Jesus leaves before the Baptism, his soul bears the
imprint of all the experiences that he had brought with him into
this incarnation.
St Paul also speaks of Christ as the second or last Adam.

So also it is written, 'The first man, Adam, became a living
soul.' The last Adam became a life-giving spirit. However,
the spiritual is not first, but the natural; then the spiritual.
The first man is from the earth, earthy; the second man
is from heaven. As is the earthy, so also are those who are
earthy; and as is the heavenly, so also are those who are
heavenly. Just as we have borne the image of the earthy, we
will also bear the image of the heavenly. (1Cor.15:45–49).

Rudolf Steiner casts light on Paul's words in his lectures
on *From Jesus to Christ*. There is a natural line of descent from
Adam, who stands as the progenitor of earthly humanity. Our
entanglement with the world that is cut off from the original
glory began in the moment when Adam ate from the 'tree of

knowledge', and developed a consciousness that cut him off from human origins in the divine. This has been the heritage of human beings since that moment. The Second Adam represents a new descent. We may re-integrate ourselves into the glory of the spiritual world and overcome the divide if we come into relationship with Christ as a new 'ancestor'. We are familiar with the stream of time that flows from the past into the future. There is also a stream of time that flows towards us from the future. When Jesus speaks of himself as 'Son of Man', or Paul speaks of him as the new Adam, we are being shown the archetype of our future becoming. The assumption of Jesus' humanity means that all human beings have been given this new, future heritage as a potential. When we consciously open ourselves for Christ, that potential starts to be realised.

In recent decades, there has been an increasing awareness that we are part of systems on many levels from the subatomic to the cosmic. A system is a whole that is greater than the sum of the parts. As human beings we are part of a system that contains all human beings, which is influenced by and influences each of its members. On the human level, whatever thoughts I am thinking, they are being thought within and on behalf of the whole of humanity. Whatever experiences I have, whatever deeds I do, are significant for the whole. This awareness of the whole of humanity as an interrelated system would have been familiar to the ancient theologians, for whom *ousia,* the substance or nature of a thing, was as real as the individuals who shared in it.

Incarnation as process

Canon Shepherd points out that our picture of the Incarnation of Christ depends on our picture of the incarnation of every human being. Neither dogmatic theology nor naturalistic science has a picture of the development towards selfhood that fits our experience. For some biologists at least, the self is an illusion created by the brain, as encapsulated the title of an article in New Scientist: 'Your mind's greatest trick is convincing you of your own reality.' Statements such as these assault the integrity of our experience as human beings. On the other hand, dogmatic religion gives an equally abstract answer when it declares the human person to be complete from the moment of conception (for example, see the Catechism of the Catholic Church, article 1703: 'Endowed with "a spiritual and immortal" soul, the human person from his conception ... is destined for eternal beatitude.') We overcome these abstractions when we see incarnation as a process. Then we will understand what it was the Logos was incarnating into.

Through his studies of Goethe, Rudolf Steiner discovered that when we look at nature with open eyes, we can discover different systems or organisations at work. We need one kind of eyes to look at inorganic nature, such as stones and minerals. If we look at a plant, we discern within a physical body a field of forces and forms that are responsible for the working of organic processes, building up and maintaining the organic form, where otherwise the earthly substances would revert to their inorganic state. These forces are what Steiner called the etheric or life-sphere. When we look at an animal, we see both of these worlds at work, but we discover too an inner realm in which experiences arise. This is the soul or astral body. And when we turn to the human being we see all of these 'bodies' combined and indwelt by an ego or I.

The gospels trace the process by which the divine Logos enters and transforms the four members of man's being one after the other. We could call this the healing of human nature 'from above', through the work of the Logos.

6. Stages of the Assumption

Thus we are shown quite clearly how the Christ-I worked upon all the other members of man's being ... The writer of the Gospel of St Luke ... wished to show how the healing influences proceeding from the I indicate the attainment of a lofty level in the evolutionary process; and he shows how Christ worked upon the astral body, the etheric body and the physical body of man.

Rudolf Steiner, According to Luke, *Sep 24, 1909*

The Incarnation is not an instant change but a continuing process of 'assumption' (see p. 76). Stage by stage, the divine Logos took on human nature and made it his own, in order to heal it. This chapter traces those stages, concentrating particularly on the beginning of the process, the assumption of the human I.

The I

Gerard Manley Hopkins' poem, which we looked at in Chapter 2, refers to our experience of shame and brokenness as the place where the immortal diamond of our true self will shine out. Hopkins was a master of finding sounds to match meaning. The final lines of his masterpiece reveal a deeper meaning:

I am all at once what Christ is, | since he was what I am, and
   This Jack, joke, poor potsherd, | patch, matchwood, immortal diamond,
   Is immortal diamond.

In the first line, 'I am' is repeated twice. We are reminded of the seven 'I am' sayings of the Gospel of St John, which reveal like a rainbow seven rays of Christ's sunlike being. Then, in the second and third lines, the I am is repeated again in the vowels of 'd-i-a-mond', a word which leads the I am over into the A-O, the Alpha and Omega, title of Christ in the Book of Revelation, which reveals him as the creator of all – the very origin and the destination of the world.

The poem points us to the deepest mystery of our earthly existence: the divine I am assumes a human I. Earthly experience with all its trials and pains can be the pressure that forms immortal diamond, the divine-human I am which is the harvest of the earth.

The Incarnation answers a need at the core of modern consciousness, which we examined above, in Chapter 1. The modern picture of the world leaves less and less space for the uniqueness of the human spirit. Only human beings' uniquely destructive potential is spoken of: the negative contribution that they can make to the development of earthly things, in the environmental crisis. A spiritual ecology, such as we outline below (p. 98) would see this destructive power as the shadow-side of a unique place in Creation. Such an idea is out of fashion. Modern human beings are strangely divided between an awareness of their power and a habit of discounting their significance. This is far more than just a theoretical problem. The only comfort on offer for the pointless destruction that we see around us is the reassurance that we are irrelevant. Beneath the self-indulgent culture of western consumerism lies nihilism – there is nothing left to do but 'eat and drink and be merry, for tomorrow we may die' (Eccles.8:15 and Isa.22:13).

However, again and again we see that this nihilism is not the deepest layer of all. In the early 1990s something remarkable happened to a quotation by Marianne Williamson, of which an extract follows (p. 190).

Our deepest fear is not that we are inadequate. Our deepest fear is that we are powerful beyond measure. It is our light not our darkness that most frightens us ... We were born to make manifest the glory of God that is within us.

There is a persistent belief that these words had been quoted or even invented by Nelson Mandela at his Inauguration as President of South Africa. It is now proved beyond doubt that this was not so. It seems to have been important for human beings to believe that these words about the reality of our power and our place in God's purposes were spoken by Nelson Mandela, who embodied the reality of 'immortal diamond'. Writing before his funeral, Bishop Desmond Tutu said, 'Prison became a crucible that burned away the dross.' The reaction to Mandela's death in December 2013 demonstrated what human beings long to be, and what they know they are in their deepest being.

When human beings discover their creative potential, they align themselves with the purposes of the divine world. The experience that we are uniquely creative as well as uniquely destructive prepares us for the insight that the creator spirits are waiting for human beings to take up their task as co-creators of a new world. Human beings are called upon to be the tenth angelic hierarchy.

> After the Archangels and Angels, the Arch-messengers and messengers, we will have to rank the Spirits of Freedom or the Spirits of Love, and this, beginning from above, is the tenth of the hierarchies, which is still in the process of development, but it belongs to the spiritual hierarchies. (*The Spiritual Hierarchies*, April 18, 1909).

The healing of the human being begins in the I. Achieving self-awareness, the I-consciousness, can shut human beings off from the spirit, but their free choice to move beyond self-enclosed existence in love is the purpose of the earth. The seed-Word within the I needed to be renewed first, because of the danger that threatened as human beings developed towards selfhood. Rudolf Steiner speaks of the Incarnation and Passion of Christ as 'literally the rescue of the human I'. (*From Jesus to Christ*, Oct 11, 1911).

Man would have become a self-aware I, but it would have
been an I that led man ever more into egotism, which
would have made love disappear from the earth. Humanity
was ripe for the development of the I, but this would
have been an empty I... Christ's achievement through his
deed on earth was to give this I its content, to propel it to
develop in such a way that by itself it could let flow from
itself the power that we call the power of love. *(According
to Luke,* Sep 25, 1909).

The change is not achieved simply through the gift being
bestowed; human beings must choose to make it their own if it is to
become fully effective. This choice is nothing less than the personal
decision to reconnect to the great circulation of glory. In the Gospels,
the glorious world of the spirit is referred to as the Kingdom of God.

If there had been no human beings at that time capable of
... establishing an active soul connection with the Christ,
all human connection with the spiritual world would
gradually have been lost and human beings would not have
accepted into their I's the connection with the kingdom
of heaven. If all the human beings living at such a crucial
time had persisted in remaining in darkness, it might have
happened that this [the Incarnation] would have passed by
them unnoticed. Then human souls would have become
withered, desolate, and depraved. To be sure, they would
have continued to incarnate for a time without the Christ,
but they would not have been able to implant in their I's
what was necessary for them to regain their connection
with the kingdom of heaven. *(The Reappearance of Christ,*
Jan 25, 1910)

We still live in the tension between developing ourselves and
living for others. In 'First World' countries this is being played
out on the scale of society, where an old ideal of social solidarity
imposed from outside has been rejected, but not yet replaced.
In the space that is waiting to be filled by an experience of the

selfless self, some human beings fall prey to the allure of self-glorification at the expense of others, manipulating markets and politics to accumulate such wealth and power that they can live in the illusion of needing no-one. They are a demonstration of where the trajectory that started with the Fall of Man would lead if there had been no other influence: to the complete atomisation of human beings and the end of common humanity.

Thankfully we can see another influence at work. Many initiatives that have grown up in the last half a century that give evidence that a new consciousness of our humanity is emerging. With the right spiritual insight, we can discern within it the emergence of the new human being, the enlightened individual who seeks cooperation with others.

> Then one can bring the right feelings towards Christ, so that he can become ever more that being that fills our own I, if we see him as the rescuer of earthly humanity from being scattered. Wherever we can perceive this unification of the whole of humanity over the earth, Christianity is there. *(Steiner, geistige Vereinigung,* Jan 9, 1916).

Just as the Logos-philosophy gave Justin the basis for a truly universal Christianity (see p. 14), this objective understanding of the work of Christ allows us to hold a picture of Christianity which extends far beyond the boundaries of the churches. If we belong to a Christian church, we can notice with humility how many of those who embody the truly Christian spirit belong to other religions or none at all. Christ is greater than the churches, indeed he is greater than the religion that bears his name. Nevertheless, celebrating 'anonymous Christians' and the anonymous Christianity that is emerging today does not mean that we should deny Christ or even stop talking about him. The strengths of the new consciousness lie in two areas: the awareness of the earth, and the awareness of the dignity of the human being, manifest in concern for human rights and social justice. However, impulses for the renewal that is needed in these areas will only flow when there is a new awareness of the spirit; of the spirit not as an alternative to earthly reality, but as the basis and hope for the earth. This could be the basis for a new sense of Christian mission, which would have little to do with telling people the name of Jesus Christ, and more to do with discovering the deep yearning that may be there with modern human beings to understand the spirit that embraces the broken world and leads it to its glorification. We will discuss this further in Chapter 7.

→ *Contemplation on having and being* ←

The aim of this contemplation is to show how a passage from the gospels can come alive when we find its relevance to our life. The story of the rich ruler in Luke 18:18–30 is a meditation on receiving and letting go.

A certain ruler asked Jesus a question. 'Good teacher,' he said, 'what must I do to receive eternal life?' 'Why do you call me good?' Jesus answered. 'No one is good except God. You know what the commandments say. "Do not commit adultery. Do not commit murder. Do not steal. Do not give false witness. Honour your father and mother".' 'I have obeyed all those commandments since I was a boy,' the ruler said. When Jesus heard this, he said to him, 'You are still missing one thing. Sell everything you have. Give the money to those who are poor. You will have treasure in heaven. Then come and follow me.' When the ruler heard this, he became very sad. He was very rich.

Perhaps this man sees his greatest 'treasure' in the fact that he can say with simple assurance, 'I have obeyed the commandments since I was a boy.' Jesus seems to agree that this is indeed so. Instead of challenging this brave assertion, Jesus reflects on something else, the man's use of the word 'good'. In English we have made a noun out of the word 'good' to mean possessions, or things we trade in – 'goods'. As soon as we try to cultivate a spiritual life, we are faced with the temptation of accumulating treasure – of *having* spiritual goods, rather than walking on the path. *Doing* the good is an activity; the fact that I may have managed a minute ago does not mean that I am now 'good'. Only one thing determines my 'goodness' in this moment – the decision I make in freedom, which may bring me into closer alignment with my own true being, and with ultimate reality. This decision is so absorbing that there is no space for any awareness of *being* good. The statement, he is good, or I am good, is essentially meaningless. I may have lived in tune with ultimate reality in the past, but that gives no guarantee of what is to come. The moment I start to make a status out of what I have achieved, I am hindered from being in the moment.

The only antidote to this is to sell everything. That means that we do not develop any qualities for ourselves, even though our self is the place in which we can develop our qualities. To be a free I means to gain treasure and give it away even before we notice that we have it.

The soul

We have seen how the I would be a pure channel for experience and a centre of initiative in line with what it experienced, if it were left to itself. Through becoming entangled in a soul-world that has been distorted by the adversary powers, it cannot unfold its pure nature. In a remarkable lecture in *The World of the Senses and the World of the Spirit* (Nov 29, 1911), Rudolf Steiner describes how each member of man's being in turn is brought into a distorted relationship with the others through the consequences of the Fall. This lecture, which contains the seeds for a pastoral theology that has yet to be fully developed, is the background for the descriptions that follow.

After the Baptism in the Jordan, Jesus experiences the Temptation. The Greek word translated as 'tempt' means to put to the test. Every problem in life has the potential to increase our capacities if we can recognise it as a test. If we remove the moralistic overtones that have grown up around the word 'temptation', we can see in the challenge by the adversary powers the necessary resistance through which our capacities can grow. The adversaries create this resistance by drawing us into one-sidedness.

In the case of the I, this distortion means that we over-identify with our own feelings, which are in turn distorted and exaggerated by the effects of the adversary powers. The I of Jesus, now permeated through and through by the divine Logos, is still a human I and is still subject to being drawn into the extremes represented by Lucifer and Ahriman.

> Jesus, full of the Holy Spirit, left the Jordan and was led by the Spirit into the wilderness, where for forty days he was tempted by the devil. He ate nothing during those days, and at the end of them he was hungry. The devil said to him, 'If you are the Son of God, tell this stone to become bread.' Jesus answered, 'It is written: *Man shall not live on bread alone.*' The devil led him up to a high place and showed him in an instant all the kingdoms of the world. And he said to him, 'I will give you all their authority and splendour; it has been given to me, and I can give it to anyone I want to. If you worship me, it will all be yours.' Jesus answered, 'It is written: *Worship the Lord your God and serve him only.*' The devil led him to Jerusalem and had him stand on the highest point of the temple. 'If you are the Son of God,' he said, 'throw yourself down from here. For it is written: *He will command his angels concerning you to guard you carefully; they will lift you up in their hands, so that you will not strike your foot against a stone.*' Jesus answered, 'It is said: *Do not put the Lord your God to the test.*' When the devil had finished all this tempting, he left him until an opportune time. (Luke 4:1–13).

In the temptation to defy gravity by throwing himself down from a pinnacle, Jesus Christ encounters the reality of the Luciferic power in the soul. All grandiosity, every inclination to believe that we are special and that the normal laws of earthly existence do not apply to us, are the bequest of Lucifer. The integrating power of the I allows us to hold the balance between the extremes, where otherwise we would swing from an exaggerated picture of our own glory to the opposite, feeling crushed under the weight of our shortcomings and failures, in which we can see the influence of Ahriman. Every tendency to judge ourselves or others, to come to a final decision on whether we, or they, are 'good' or 'bad' people, shows that we have not found the power of the I in the centre of the soul. In its essential being, the I simply describes the world, and does not need to judge it.

In the temptation to fall down and worship the tempter we can see a collaboration between the two forces – Lucifer shows the vast, enticing prospect; Ahriman makes clear the reality of earthly power. This is the temptation that anyone in a position of leadership feels – it is easy to imagine the world that my leadership could bring about; easy too to compromise on the means to get there. The commandment to worship only God is greater than an instruction concerning which power amongst many competing ones the Israelites should choose. Rather, it points to the fact that we will not find fulfilment when what we do is aligned to any other reality than ultimate reality itself.

In the temptation to turn stones into bread we see above all the influence of Ahriman, who would reduce all human life to 'stones', the satisfaction of merely material needs. Rudolf Steiner points out that Jesus was unable to answer this temptation fully; after all, the power of hunger is not wiped out by the fact that food is not the *only* thing that we need to live. The divine Logos has not yet comprehended the harsh reality of human existence for which purely spiritual nourishment is not sufficient. All the stages of the Incarnation including the full assumption of the physical body are necessary before he can give an 'answer', which is in fact his deed of sacrifice. This inaugurates a new humanity, one which is not condemned to separation but can find the way to its spiritual source, from which a new kind of nourishment can flow. The temptation will only be fully answered once that new humanity has come to birth.

Jesus' responses to the adversaries are a living embodiment of the sovereign I. Whether intentionally or not, the way that a question or a challenge is framed contains a suggestive power which seeks to compel me to answer in the same terms. This can be crass, as for example when an interviewer on the radio says, 'So tell me, minister, when did your government decide to discriminate against the disadvantaged?' It can be subtler, such as when someone tries to persuade us with strong feeling. We can respond to this by shutting ourselves off. However, if true conversation is to take place, our soul needs to flow into the soul-world of the one speaking with us. Then we need to return to ourselves. Our I needs to stand apart from what we are experiencing. When we cultivate our inner life, we gradually learn to say to ourselves not 'I feel' or even 'I think', but, 'My soul is feeling; my soul is thinking'. Only then are we free to decide what *we ourselves* – our I – wish to do with these thoughts and feelings. This is inner leadership, which is at the root of all effective outer leadership. In meeting the challenge of the Adversaries and remaining sovereign, Jesus Christ implants this possibility in the human soul.

Nourishment

Qualities of inner leadership that give strength in dealing with the challenges of their destiny allow some people to radiate a power that can help and nourish those around them. In her book, *The Hiding Place,* Corrie ten Boom describes how she was able to smuggle in a bottle of vitamins when she and her sister were taken off to a concentration camp. At the time they entered Ravensbrück, the bottle was about half full. Vitamin deficiency was one of the worst hazards to prisoners, and Corrie's instinct was to hoard the precious vial for her sister Betsie, who was malnourished and ill. But Betsie wouldn't allow her to hoard it for her. They could not say no 'to eyes that burned with fever, hands that shook with chill,' Corrie writes. Soon there were more than thirty people receiving a daily dose, and still, 'every time I tilted the little bottle, a drop appeared at the top of the stopper. Many times I lay awake trying to fathom the marvel of supply lavished upon us.' (p. 97) The day a new bottle of vitamin supplements arrived from the Red Cross, the little bottle was empty.

We learn from the book that Betsie had achieved a remarkable degree of inner transformation. It is possible to imagine that she was able so to extend her soul so that it could touch the souls of those around her. They experienced the abundance of her soul-life, and this potentised the tiny drop or even the fragrance from the bottle, so that they experienced that they got what they needed. The experience was so powerful that it had a physiological effect. There are many similar stories, both in the Bible and in modern accounts of human beings sharing great hardship. Nowadays, the fact that physiological changes can be caused by our state of soul is accepted in psycho-somatic medicine, and in the placebo effect.

The gospels show how Jesus' soul became nourishment for those who streamed towards him once the Word had brought it into harmony.

Jesus crossed to the far shore of the Sea of Galilee (that is, the Sea of Tiberias), and a great crowd of people followed him because they saw the signs he had performed by healing those who were ill. Then Jesus went up on a mountainside and sat down with his disciples. The Jewish Passover Festival was near.

When Jesus looked up and saw a great crowd coming towards him, he said to Philip, 'Where shall we buy bread for these people to eat?' He asked this only to test him, for he already had in mind what he was going to do.

Philip answered him, 'It would take more than half a year's wages to buy enough bread for each one to have a bite!'

Another of his disciples, Andrew, Simon Peter's brother, spoke up, 'Here is a boy with five small barley loaves and two small fish, but how far will they go among so many?'

Jesus said, 'Make the people sit down.' There was plenty of grass in that place, and they sat down (about five thousand men were there). Jesus then took the loaves, gave thanks, and distributed to those who were seated as much as they wanted. He did the same with the fish.

When they had all had enough to eat, he said to his disciples, 'Gather the pieces that are left over. Let nothing be wasted.' So they gathered them and filled twelve baskets with the pieces of the five barley loaves left over by those who had eaten. (John 6:1–13).

This experience of abundant nourishment where it was not expected could seem to contradict Jesus' refusal to turn stones into bread in the Temptation. A closer reading shows us that there is no need to visualise a physical multiplication of the loaves and fishes; in fact, it is very hard to imagine how such miraculously produced food could have been shared out among 5,000 men and their dependants in a manageable length of time. Rather, we can imagine that food that has passed through the hands of Jesus, who has given thanks (*eucharistein* in Greek) contains within it a power to nourish that far surpasses its physical nutritional value. If we picture the distribution of the loaves, we may imagine that the very quality of this holy food awakens selflessness, as everyone wants to leave enough bread to pass on to their neighbour. So when the twelve disciples go round with their baskets, every group that has divided a small part of the loaf among itself has something left over. The whole scene is a prophecy of the new humanity which will provide the final answer to the temptation to turn stones into bread.

The depths

In some icons from the early days of Christianity, the Baptism is portrayed not only as the moment when the Holy Spirit descended from above, but as the moment when the depths opened up and a river-monster emerged. This monster embodied the chaos and destruction that resided in the 'deeps'. This image recalls the story of Creation in Genesis 1 which is as a struggle between the progressive creator spirits and the retrograde spirits at work in the chaos of the waters. The life of Jesus Christ is more than a recapitulation of human experience: it is a recapitulation of Creation itself.

Through the twentieth century, humanity became ever more aware of the 'depths' of the human soul – unconscious drives and motivations which have the power to engulf our souls like the waves on a stormy sea. Unfortunately, not everything that has been done in the name of the unconscious is helpful on our path to freedom. However, we can become students of our life of soul, noticing what happens from the sovereign standpoint of our free I. Then we can learn to distinguish different forces at work and their power.

For example, if we try to live our lives by spiritual ideals, we are exposed to the Luciferic temptation: we think that we have already overcome all the emotions and drives that we see as 'bad'. It is not comfortable to experience anger; even less comfortable is the recognition that I an angry person who can be hurtful to others. However, divorcing ourselves from deep emotions such as this is both dangerous and wasteful. The danger comes from the fact that what we cannot own has the greater power over us – we make it into the monster that we fear. The waste happens because these forces are a part of our power, and if we can integrate them they can help us to achieve our aims. If I can bear to recognise that I am angry, then I can discover what I am angry about. I gain useful information about the deeper regions of my soul. I am then free to decide how to act on what I have learned. I may need to find a way to vent the anger before I plan how to bring about the changes the anger was trying to effect. A healthy soul-life integrates what surges up from the depths and guides it into constructive pathways.

When Jesus walks on the water after the feeding of the five thousand, and when he has the power to still the storm, the sovereign self-leadership of the Logos has extended into the deepest realms of the soul.

Life

After the divine Logos had taken hold of Jesus' soul, he came ever more into relationship with the field of forces that lift the processes of life from the realm of inorganic nature into their own sphere. Rudolf Steiner refers to this field as the life or etheric body. 'Body' here clearly bears an extended meaning – it is a contained field of forces that work together.

In the story of Adam's sojourn in Paradise and the subsequent Fall, two trees are given particular mention: the Tree of Life and the Tree of Knowledge. Adam was told that he might eat fruit from all the trees except the Tree of Knowledge. Before his eyes were opened and he saw himself separate from his creative origin, Adam was embedded the spiritual world. The knowing resulting from eating of the Tree of Knowledge meant that he experienced himself separate from the world, and this cut him off from the source of life:

> And the Lord God said, 'The man has now become like
> one of us, knowing good and evil. He must not be allowed
> to reach out his hand and take also from the tree of life
> and eat, and live for ever.' So the Lord God banished him
> from the Garden of Eden to work the ground from which
> he had been taken. (Gen 3:22f).

The knowledge of good and evil is the beginning of the human journcy towards independent selfhood. If we take the detail about the Tree of Life as an objective description rather than a personal punishment, we can see that this kind of knowing cuts us off from the living world of our origins. Rudolf Steiner describes with precise concepts what the Bible presents in mythological pictures.

> Imagine that the Luciferic temptation had never taken
> place; after death, human beings would leave behind a
> far more rejuvenated ether body, a much 'greener' ether
> body, as it were. Because of the Luciferic temptation,
> human beings leave behind a far more dried-up ether body

than would have otherwise been the case. *(Die geistige Vereinigung,* Dec 28, 1915).

The journey away from our origin is the journey into death. When Jesus walked on the water, the divine Logos had arrived in the sphere of life. The Transfiguration shows what happens when the assumption of the etheric body is complete:

And after six days Jesus took with him Peter and James and John his brother, and led them up a high mountain apart. And he was transfigured before them, and his face shone like the sun, and his garments became white as light. And behold, there appeared to them Moses and Elijah, talking with him. And Peter said to Jesus, 'Lord, it is well that we are here; if you wish, I will make three booths here, one for you and one for Moses and one for Elijah.' He was still speaking, when lo, a bright cloud overshadowed them, and a voice from the cloud said, 'This is my beloved Son, with whom I am well pleased; listen to him.' When the disciples heard this, they fell on their faces, and were filled with awe. But Jesus came and touched them, saying, 'Rise, and have no fear.' And when they lifted up their eyes, they saw no one but Jesus only. And as they were coming down the mountain, Jesus commanded them, 'Tell no one the vision, until the Son of man is raised from the dead.' (Matt 17:1–9)

The life-body has been irradiated with a new power.

The instant in which the etheric body of Jesus of Nazareth (in which Christ then was) had become capable of imbuing the physical body with new life in the fullest sense, in that instant the etheric body of Christ appears transfigured. *(The Gospel of St John,* July 5, 1909).

The Transfiguration is also the moment when the etheric body becomes the germ of the restoration of the physical body:

And Christ speaks of what had happened, saying, Now is
the judgment of this world; now shall the Prince of this
world be cast out. Lucifer-Ahriman was cast out of the
physical body of Christ in that moment. ... Man's physical
body must be so enlivened by the impulse of Christ that
the fruits of the mission of the Earth may be carried over
into the times which will follow the Earth-period. *(The
Gospel of St John,* July 5, 1909).

The transformed soul of Jesus became nourishment for the
hungry souls in the feeding of the five thousand. After the
Transfiguration, the corresponding deed is the healing of a boy
whom we might today call epileptic.

When they came to the crowd, a man approached Jesus
and knelt before him. 'Lord, have mercy on my son,' he
said. 'He has seizures and is suffering greatly. He often
falls into the fire or into the water. I brought him to your
disciples, but they could not heal him.' 'You unbelieving
and perverse generation,' Jesus replied, 'how long shall I
stay with you? How long shall I put up with you? Bring
the boy here to me.' Jesus rebuked the demon, and it came
out of the boy, and he was healed at that moment. Then
the disciples came to Jesus in private and asked, 'Why
couldn't we drive it out?' He replied, 'Because you have
so little faith. Truly I tell you, if you have faith as small
as a mustard seed, you can say to this mountain, "Move
from here to there," and it will move. Nothing will be
impossible for you.' (Matt.17:14–20)

The gospels places this healing immediately after the
Transfiguration, thus pointing us to the connection between
the two events. In his artistic genius, Raphael showed them
happening simultaneously in his picture of the Transfiguration.
On the mountain-top, Christ appears in his sunlike radiance;
down below, in an eerie, moonlike light, the drama of the healing
of the boy unfolds. The link between the two scenes is implied by

their being painted on the same canvas. In the gospel text, the link is formed by Jesus' coming down from the heights and touching the disciples, who are overwhelmed by what they see, and leading them down into the depths where the healing will happen.

When we learn that the dwelling place of the Logos during the creation of the earth was the Sun, we can sense the temptation to stay in the sunlit realm of the Transfiguration. Rudolf Steiner describes how as the spirit of the sun, bestower of life and the natural home of the etheric body, the Logos felt the magnetic pull of the purified life body to leave the earth behind. It is his compassion, first for the disciples and then for the boy, that anchors him on the earth.

In the words Jesus speaks about the healing, we can sense that the disorder and therefore its healing are rooted in the sphere of life. In the Gospel of St Mark, Jesus tells the disciples that such a demon 'can come out only by prayer' (9:29). Only through the cultivation of an inner life can we create a new body of habits and change our life-body; this outwardly invisible activity is a seed that grows within us and becomes a source of life.

The body

The church fathers perceived that the physical body itself was in danger of corruption. Like an icon that has grown dirty through years of standing in front of the candles on the altar, the image of God, the archetypal image of human nature, has been overlaid with soot. Only the Word can restore the image, of which he was both the original and the artist.

> For as, when the likeness painted on a panel has been
> effaced by stains from without, he whose likeness it is,
> must needs come once more to enable the portrait to
> be renewed on the same wood – in the same way also
> the most holy Son of the Father, being the Image of the
> Father, came to our region to renew man once made in
> His likeness, and find him, as one lost, by the remission of

sins; as He says Himself in the Gospels: 'I came to find and to save the lost.' ... For this purpose, then, the incorporeal and incorruptible and immaterial Word of God entered our world ... taking a body like our own, because all our bodies were liable to the corruption of death, He surrendered His body to death instead of all, and offered it to the Father ... This He did that He might turn again to incorruption men who had turned back to corruption, and make them alive through death by the appropriation of His body and by the grace of His resurrection. Thus He would make death to disappear from them as utterly as straw from fire. (Athanasius, *De Incarnatione*, 8).

Rudolf Steiner places the insight of the early theologians into the context of the development of humanity.

They beheld concretely in spirit what would have happened ... namely, that human physical bodies would have deteriorated so much that the whole future of humanity would have been endangered. *(Die menschliche Seele,* May 7, 1923).

The original circulation of glory was interrupted so that a world could emerge that was not a pure reflection of the divine world. Only in the balance of forces in the physical world can human beings develop towards freedom. The point of earth-evolution is to provide the conditions in which the human I can develop. This means that the I must incarnate fully in a physical body. Only through this can human beings' decision to become co-creators be real.

The physical body then is the field on which the mission of the earth can be fulfilled. It is a mirror which is the foundation for our immediate experience of ourselves. This is the counterpart to the awareness of self that is built on past experiences. We saw above that the 'I' lives between what it perceives and what it does. For both of these, we rely on the physical body: our sense-organs allow us to perceive the world; our limbs and hands are the instruments through which we can move through the world and affect it. Had it become impossible for us to incarnate on the earth, the plans of the divine world would have been thwarted. Using the term 'Mystery of Golgotha', which for him sums up the Incarnation, Passion and Resurrection of Christ, Steiner describes how the assumption of the physical body by the divine Logos restores the body and enables human development to continue:

> The human physical body itself was imbued again with the necessary forces of life and freshness. Human beings were thereby enabled to continue their further evolution on earth, inasmuch as they could now come down from worlds of spirit-and-soul and find it possible to live in physical bodies. Such was the actual effect of the Mystery of Golgotha. *(Die menschliche Seele,* May 7, 1923).

We have become accustomed to the thought that bad decisions made by human beings can be damaging for the earth. This awareness has led to a perception that the earth is a living being. Ecological awareness usually goes hand in hand with a rejection of the idea of human supremacy. Awareness of the damage that human beings have caused makes it hard for many people to imagine that they have a special place in creation. A spiritual ecology would embrace the idea that the earth's purpose is bound up with the destiny of mankind. For such a way of thinking, the living being of the earth would suffer if the human body were irredeemably corrupted. Rudolf Steiner speaks about this danger, which was averted through the death and resurrection of Jesus Christ.

> But Christ through his dwelling in Jesus of Nazareth, has healed this physical body so that it is no longer harmful to the earth's existence; and we can calmly look down into earthly existence knowing that after the mystery of Golgotha bad seed is not falling into the earth with the physical body that the human being otherwise needs for the development of the I. And so Christ passed through

the mystery of Golgotha in order to heal and sanctify the human physical body for the earth. *(The Mystery of the Trinity,* July 30, 1922).

Freedom in the body

In the descriptions of the Holy Week in the Gospels, we are confronted with the reality of the physical body of Jesus: we witness him being anointed, kissed, stripped, whipped, crowned with thorns, burdened under the weight of the cross, and crucified. These events taken together are referred to as the Passion of Christ. Passion comes from the same root as our words passive and patient. The divine Logos suffers himself to be fully at one with the reality of human existence. The silence with which he rides into Jerusalem continues when he is being mocked and tortured in the night of Maundy Thursday. This is not the silence of impassiveness, however, as if he were detached from what is going on. When confronted with the snaring questions of the religious leaders on the Tuesday of Holy Week, he meets their demands with his own, and betters them in debate (see for example Matt.22:15–45). And he expresses his compassion with those who weep for him, even as he is carrying the cross to Golgotha.

We witness the free relationship of a sovereign I to all the members of his being. The free I knows that it is separate from the soul, as we saw above (p. 92). In the Garden of Gethsemane, Jesus says: 'My soul is overwhelmed with sorrow to the point of death. Stay here and keep watch with me' (Matt.26:38). The word he uses is *psyche*, which in Greek means both soul and life. The bright flame of the Logos cannot burn long in a human being without using up the forces of life available. Then comes the moment when with fiery resolve he prays for strength to withstand whatever may come, using words that remind us of the prayer of the free I, the Lord's Prayer: 'My Father, if this cannot pass unless I drink it, your will be done' (Matt.26:42).

Finally in the scenes on the cross, we witness the sovereign

I undimmed even as the body is dying. He is concerned for his
mother and the beloved disciple; he gives an answer to the robber
who shows some understanding of what has happened; he asks for
forgiveness for those who crucify him, 'for they know not what
they do' (Luke 23:34).

First-born from the dead

The Holy Week is rich in images. Jesus enters Jerusalem riding
an ass, an image of the physical body. We have seen that the
entry into the city is an image of the Incarnation itself. There
is the symbolic cursing of the fig-tree, and the demonstrative
action in the temple courtyard, when Jesus overturns the tables of
the traders. Every action that Jesus took during his life on earth
bore deeper meaning; in the Holy Week, the saturation with
meaning takes on a new intensity. The healing of one human
nature is played out in the sense-perceptible sphere, so that the
eyes of other human beings might see it. The renewal of the
seed-Word starts with a demonstration. This reaches its climax in
the Crucifixion, where the Logos, now united with humanity, is
displayed for all to see. John reminds us that this was prophesied
as part of what would happen to the Messiah: 'And again another
passage of scripture says, *They will look on the one whom they have
pierced*' (John 19:37).

Rudolf Steiner echoes this in his contemplation of the
Crucifixion in his lectures on Gospel of St Luke.

> Saint Luke has set before us this great Ideal of evolution:
> 'Look towards your future! Your I, in the present stage
> of its development, is still weak; as yet it has little
> mastery. But it will gradually become master of the astral
> body, the etheric body and the physical body, and will
> transform them. Before you is set the great Ideal of Christ
> who reveals to mankind what this mastery can mean!'
> (*According to Luke,* Sep 24, 1909).
> The culmination of the process of penetrating and taking on

the members of a human being is an appearance: an epiphany. The Christian path of knowing starts when human beings behold outside of them as historical fact what they are destined to become. What human beings perceive on the cross is the prototype of a new kind of life. As the modern theologian Frances Young puts it (p. 85):

> Necessarily [salvation] implies the resurrection of the body, the restoration of the whole person by the creative power of God. The creedal doctrine of the resurrection of the flesh affirms that the bodily existence of humanity is to be healed and restored along with its moral and spiritual being ...

Both Paul and the writer of the Book of Revelation refer again and again to Christ as the first-born from the dead. His death makes a new kind of living and dying possible. Rudolf Steiner uses the word 'phantom' to describe the pure form of the physical body, which is a reality even before it clads itself with material. The 'corruption' which the early theologians perceived comes when the spiritual archetype of the physical body clads itself with matter from the divided world. The progressive transformation of the members of Jesus' being means that the pure form is unclouded.

> When this body of Jesus of Nazareth was fastened to the cross, the Phantom was perfectly intact; it existed in a spiritual bodily form, visible only to supersensible sight, and was much more loosely connected with the body's material content of earth-elements than has ever happened with any other human being ... When the body was taken down from the cross, the parts were still coherent, but they had no connection with the Phantom; the Phantom was completely free of them. When the body became permeated with certain substances, which in this case worked quite differently from the way in which they affect any other body that is embalmed, it came to pass that

after the burial the material parts quickly volatilised and passed over into the elements. Hence the disciples who looked into the grave found the linen cloths in which the body had been wrapped, but the Phantom, on which the evolution of the I depends, had risen from the grave. *(From Jesus to Christ,* Oct 12, 1911).

7. Bringing Christ to Life Within Us

Let us seek to be like Christ, because Christ also became like us: to become gods through him since he himself, through us, became a man. He took the worst upon himself to make us a gift of the best.

Gregory of Nazianzus Orationes *1, 5: SC 247, 78*

The Incarnation changed what it can mean to be human. The event of two thousand years ago affects our reality today.

Following Christ

There are moments when we seem to grow beyond ourselves. For example, in moments of crisis we find strength and resources that we never dreamed we might have. Something higher streams through us. We forget our everyday concerns. Thoughts and worries that have plagued us fade into the background of our awareness. All self-consciousness, vanity and preoccupation with what others may be thinking recede. We often remember such moments better than any other times of our life.

There is another, very different kind of experience of taking leave of ourselves: we can grow intoxicated by something outside of ourselves, such as a person, a group or a cause. It can be very attractive if someone seems to know all the answers and can provide certainty and a clear direction, particularly if we feel insecure in a new group, or a new situation in life. Charismatic leaders and 'gurus' trade on this. The brainwashing practised by cults, where the individual is completely obliterated and taken over by the group, is an extreme form of this. Even in less extreme circumstances, we still lose our connection with the central core of our being.

These two modes of moving beyond self are quite different, even though they are easily confused. The state of healthy self-forgetfulness moves us beyond the narrow limits of our earthly self, but in doing so brings us into connection with our true being, the self we are yet to realise on the earth. The intoxicating loss of self takes us back to a time before we were endowed with a self. In our individual development, this was infancy, when we had not yet grown separate from the world around us. In human history, it was the state of human souls in far-distant ages, when initiates, kings or pharaohs bore the purposes of their peoples, and the masses were mere drones.

It is striking that we do not have a word that conveys the realisation of our true self. We normally use the word 'selfless'. But surely this is not what we should be striving for. If we substitute the word 'I' for self, this becomes clearer: would we want to be 'I-less'? 'Selfish', on the other hand, is only negative, relating to the unredeemed lower self. Both these words show that we are uncomfortable with our greatest challenge: to discover a 'selfless self'.

The attitudes enshrined in the words 'selfless' and 'selfish' are reflected in our culture. Consumer culture tells us that the lower self and its desires are all, and encourages the cultivation of selfishness. Others preach salvation through self-abnegation. Perhaps if we found a word that expresses being what I truly am, without becoming a slave to my lower self, we would find it easier to achieve it.

Gerard Manley Hopkins meditated on the relationship between the self and Christ in this poem without a title.

As kingfishers catch fire, dragonflies draw flame;
As tumbled over rim in roundy wells
Stones ring; like each tucked string tells, each hung bell's
Bow swung finds tongue to fling out broad its name;
Each mortal thing does one thing and the same:
Deals out that being indoors each one dwells;

Selves – goes itself; *myself* it speaks and spells,
Crying *Whát I dó is me: for that I came.*

I say móre: the just man justices;
Keeps grace: thát keeps all his goings graces;
Acts in God's eye what in God's eye he is –
Chríst – for Christ plays in ten thousand places,
Lovely in limbs, and lovely in eyes not his
To the Father through the features of men's faces.

If this poem ended with the line 'Crying Whát I dó is me: for that I came,' it could be seen as an invitation to human beings to develop unbridled egotism – to be nothing but self-ish, in the normal sense of the word. In the second stanza, the poet's deeper meaning shines through. The word 'justice', which Hopkins turns into a verb, meant in New Testament times to live in accord with the Law of Moses. Now that the Law has been written into our hearts, we could say that to 'justice' means to live in alignment with the ultimate reality of our true being and of the world. This means that we emulate Jesus and try to ascend to union with our true self. 'Grace' on the other hand means a gift that we receive unearned; 'keeping grace' means to be open for the gift of the Logos who is at work in our deepest being. We can try to allow this grace to flow in our conduct in life – our 'goings graces'.

To live out of our true self means to reveal Christ. Beyond self-ish and self-less there is self-filled, which proves to be Christ-filled.

'Not I but Christ in me'

The experience of the self that is filled with Christ is at the centre of Paul's Christianity.

For through the Law I died to the Law, that I might live
unto God. I have been crucified with Christ, and it is
no longer I who live, but Christ lives in me; and the life

which I now live in the flesh I live by faith in the Son of God, who loved me and delivered Himself up for me. (Gal.2:19f).

The phrase from the Bible that Rudolf Steiner quotes far more than any other is a shortened version of these words: 'Not I, but Christ in me.' If this lights up as an ideal for us, we can see Jesus as our forerunner and guide.

> It was he who brought [grace] – he, who in the beginning of our age had the whole of Christ within himself, who was the first to fulfil and realise the whole principle of humanity. Christ Jesus made himself into that which is to live in every single human being. Through him there came into the world what can come about through freedom and peaceful cooperation. *(The Christian Mystery,* March 17, 1907).

We share this aim with Jesus. In this sense he is our model. But if we tried to imitate the way that Jesus achieved this, we would have to strive for what the Definition of Chalcedon called the 'hypostatic union' and give up being individuals. We would no longer be the centre of initiative in our own being; our identity would be that of the incarnate Logos. This is not what Hopkins expresses so beautifully in the first part of the poem when he writes 'Each mortal thing ... Selves – goes itself; *myself* it speaks and spells.'

We have seen how Jesus renounces becoming an earthly self. His humanity remains pure and archetypal. He does not develop an earthly I-consciousness and so he does not become an individualised, earthly human being. If we wished to emulate this, we would need to remain paradisal, unsullied by earthly experience. There are times when we feel burdened by the weight of our mistakes and shortcomings, when we long for this. Ultimately, though, we would feel cheated if our errors, with all their potential for learning and growth, were simply wiped out. To strive to repeat this kind of union with Christ would contradict the mission of the Incarnation, which is a great 'yes' to the path of human beings on earth. Christ did not want to divert human beings from their path but to empower them to complete it.

> Christ wished [human beings] to remain in the world and yet find salvation. He had no wish that they should return to the time before the Fall, but that they should experience the further stages of Earth evolution and yet participate in the Kingdom of Heaven. *(Building Stones,* April 10, 1917).

In relation to the I, this mission had a very specific quality:

> [Christ] wanted to dwell within humanity, but he did not want to cloud the emerging I-consciousness of human beings. He had done that once in Jesus, in whom in the place of the I-consciousness the Son-consciousness lived from the Baptism. But this was not to happen with human beings of times to come. In the case of human beings of times to come, the I was to be elevated and Christ was to dwell within them nevertheless. *(The Mystery of the Trinity,* July 30, 1922).

Meditating on what unites us with Jesus and what differentiates us, we can realise that the Incarnation itself has brought about the change. When the Logos assumed human nature transformed it, what was previously outside has now drawn into the human being. The seed-Word has been renewed, and our nature has been joined with the world of glory in a new way. We are now called upon to become the one person uniting two natures, as the Logos did in the case of Jesus Christ.

Still the images of the dynamic of assumption of the I are relevant to us, not in the same way that they worked for Jesus, but as archetypal gestures for welcoming in the Logos, who awakens the seed-Word within us. We can look once more at the Contemplation on the I of Jesus (see page 74) and think of our own experiences of 'negative capability', when our I approaches the state of the 'empty sphere' of Jesus; we can think too of experiences of being filled with the warmth of love or inspiration that is greater than our own. The third moment in the dynamic has particular relevance for us, when we think of how we are called to make Christ real within ourselves.

Can all of this help us to understand the words: 'Not I, but Christ in me'? In the lecture quoted above, Rudolf Steiner looks at this phrase in a detailed way.

> If the Christians had become aware of the Christ
> within them, they would have had to extinguish their
> I-consciousness whenever they wanted to be good, in order
> to awaken the Christ within themselves. Not they would
> have been good, but merely Christ within them would
> have been good. Human beings would have had to wander
> about on the earth; the Christ would have had to dwell in
> them, and by Christ's using human bodies, the healing of
> these bodies would have taken place. But the good deeds
> which human beings would have done would have been
> deeds of Christ, not deeds of human beings.

Being indwelt by Christ does not mean returning to the state before we had an I. Clearly, we are not supposed to strive for the state that Jesus was in, where his awareness of himself was dimmed. When we think of Christ playing 'to the Father through the features of men's faces' in Hopkins' poem, it would not be right to imagine that those human beings are aware of Christ. They are aware of themselves; of their true selves, of their deepest purpose, and of their fellow human beings. This is the gift of the Holy Spirit, the bringer of awareness and connection that is given at Whitsun.

> [Christ] sent human beings the divine being who does not
> extinguish ego-consciousness, to whom one raises oneself
> not in seeing but in the spirit which does not see. He sent
> human beings the Holy Spirit. Thus it is the Holy Spirit
> who is to be sent by the Christ, in order that man can

retain his I-consciousness and the Christ can dwell within man unconsciously. *(The Mystery of the Trinity,* July 30, 1922).

The Holy Spirit has been described as the 'reticent God'. He is the light that makes the Trinity manifest. If we think of light, it has the paradoxical quality that enables us to see, whilst itself remaining invisible. Even when we think we can see light, we are in fact seeing its meeting with darkness, for instance the dust and water droplets in the air that allows us to see beams of light shining through clouds.

Through the Incarnation, humanity has been reconnected to its origin. Being 'filled' with Christ does not mean replacing a part of ourselves with something foreign to us. It means finding healing in the very kernel of our being, the centre of our initiative and experience: our I.

To seek God and the original divine being, not in the sheath of the soul, but in the actual I – that was the contribution of Christianity, of the Christ-impulse to human development ... The entry of the divine consciousness that speaks through the I, is the essence of the Christ-impulse. *(Christ and the Twentieth Century,* Jan 25, 1912).

Finding our own law

One attitude to doing the right thing is that it will always be the choice that is most painful and unpleasant for us. What we would instinctively prefer is bound to be sinful, so we need to choose the opposite. However, if Christ dwells within the core of our being, within our I itself, then the question we need to ask is surely, 'What would I do? What do I really want?'

This can seem a shocking thought. What would it mean if everyone were allowed to do whatever they wanted? Would it not lead to anarchy, the breakdown of social order? In the face of evil deeds and crime, we sometimes find ourselves wishing for retribution or social control. It is an understandable reflex when want to protect our loved ones and ourselves from harm.

Over recent years there has been a movement to recover the ancient idea of 'restorative justice'. This seeks to address the harm suffered by victims of crime in an holistic way. Instead of removing the offender from the equation by locking him or her away, perpetrators and victims are encouraged where possible to meet and to explore the harm done and how it can be healed.

There are many stories of transformation in perpetrators of crime who were confronted for the first time by the human being whom they have terrorised, for example through theft or vandalism. Through skilled and careful mediation, the capacity to empathise with their victim grows in them. They discover that they could only commit their crime because the reality of the situation was hidden from them, or because they were acting out of something that was not part of their true being. They start to wish that they could have been true to themselves. A psychologist, Ruth Henderson, describes a client's journey to empathy and personal transformation:

> Suffering from paranoid schizophrenia, 'Ed' had killed his father in the midst of a paranoid delusion. The courts found him not guilty by reason of insanity and sent him to Bridgewater, where he was given anti-psychotic drugs that worked miracles for him.
>
> The medication cleared his mind profoundly, and he awoke to the reality of what he had done. I have never met a person more deeply remorseful ...
>
> Ed took full responsibility for what he had done. He understood he couldn't blame his mental illness for killing his father ...
>
> He came to recognize he had hated his father. The more I learned about his upbringing, it was not hard to understand why ... While he came to understand his father's behaviour was sick, he never used it to excuse or justify what he had done. In fact, he also had some love for his father and

grieved the fact he had taken away his life – grieved that there was no way to make restitution to him now.

The only place Ed found consolation was in helping his fellow patients – serving them from a place of profound empathy. Whether it was in helping a delusional man dress himself in the morning or giving cigarettes to a guy who ran out a week before he'd have money to buy more, Ed looked around and acted on his compassion for those worse off than he was. The only way he could live with himself was through empathic giving. It is this empathy that allows me to make sense of the fact Ed had copied the following words into his journal and used them as a meditation:

The growth of a person is the progressive liberation of desire. The liberation of desire, is not getting what I want, but coming to want what ultimately, I am (Moore, *Jesus the Liberator of Desire*).

Astonishing words for a murderer to want to contemplate. I think they inspired him because of the compassion he had for himself. He could have compassion for himself because he knew himself not only to be a person who hated, but someone who loved. He was confident of the love he had inside himself, and this empathic love made life meaningful.

It is natural to feel the concern that if we stop threatening ourselves and each other with outer punishment, we will be faced with anarchy, because everyone will do what they want. However, Ed discovered that when he had no control of his impulse to kill, he was not doing what he wanted, but exactly the opposite: he was doing what he did not want. What he longed for was to be his true self. This self, which is one with Christ, knows no selfishness and anger. We need to take account of the fact that we are not yet able to live out of our true ideals all the time. But if we do not allow ourselves to see the destination towards which we are striving, how can we hope to get there? Knowing the destination also means that we can work towards it, addressing that part in each of us that can become its own lawgiver.

Sin

The old attitude to sin is that there is a right and a wrong thing to do in any situation, and if we choose the wrong one, we have sinned and must bear the consequences. The root of this view is a pessimistic attitude about our Fall from unity with the divine world. We were once in a state of grace, and we fell into a state of sin. Only by being forgiven may we return to a 'state of grace' again and so be saved.

This old theology of sin has left powerful traces in our culture. Its influence is felt even by those who know nothing of the church, for example when we see life as being about doing the 'right thing'. This preoccupation can grow so strong that we dare not take a new step for fear of 'getting it wrong.'

There is an another way of looking at life. We can choose to see every moment as a unique opportunity which has been delivered to us by all the moments that have gone before. These moments include many things that we might think of as mistakes, and many others where we were more aligned with our true aims. All of them – particularly those that have brought pain to ourselves or to others – give us opportunities to learn things, which can flow into the decision we make in this moment about what we want to do now. We take leave of the picture of an angry God whose plans for us have been thwarted, or a universe which is a set of tests of whether we can 'get it right'. Creation becomes for us the infinitely risky process through which human beings may decide in freedom to choose life, to develop love, and to become creative, each in their own unique way. Our challenge is at once greater and more real. We are only required to get to know ourselves and the world better and better; to learn.

> Christ is a God who does not work in such a way that his impulses absolutely must be followed. One follows them only when one understands them, and in freedom. He is, therefore, the God who never seeks to hinder the free development of the I in this or that direction. The Christ says in the very highest sense: 'You will know the truth and

the truth will make you free.' *(The Spiritual Hierarchies,*
April 18, 1909).

Our decision to exercise freedom is part of the cosmic drama:

If the ... Father had not at one time permitted the Luciferic
influences to come to man, man would not have developed
the free I. With the Luciferic influence, the conditions for
the free I were established. That had to be permitted by the
Father-God. But just as the I, for the sake of freedom, had
to become entangled in matter, so then, in order that the
I might be freed from this entanglement, the entire love of
the Son had to lead to the Act of Golgotha. Through this
alone the freedom of man, the complete dignity of man,
first became possible. *(From Jesus to Christ,* Oct 14, 1911).

The Fall of Man, which echoes the Fall of the angels in the
spiritual world, is no longer just a curse. It is the 'happy fault' or
felix culpa, which is sung in Catholic Mass as part of the Easter
Vigil. Human beings were made as they are so that they might
become co-creators with the angelic beings and offer something
back to their creator that surpasses the first creation.

There is a value in our earthly path far greater than we can
imagine. Our errors are a part of what makes us the unique
persons that we are. The things with which we have wrestled in
our souls can become seed-beds of true wisdom. When we have
overcome our failings, they are not erased, nor should we want
them to be. The image of the immortal diamond, which we
looked at in the first chapter of the book, embodies this reality.
Diamonds are formed from carbon – one of the most common
substances on the earth, which we know as dust and dirt, as well as
coal. Under conditions of unimaginable heat and pressure, deep
below the earth's crust, this commonplace material is pressed into
the clear, hard gemstone, an image of perfection and eternity.

In his book, *How to Know Higher Worlds,* Rudolf Steiner
describes the meeting with the Guardian of the Threshold, a
terrifying figure who guards the entry to the spiritual world.

This Guardian reveals himself as the result of everything within our being that we have not yet owned and transformed through our conscious efforts. At first we shrink back from this figure in horror; gradually, though, it becomes clear that he bears a gift: the possibility of cooperating in our redemption through self knowledge.

> The student's preparation must aim at enabling him
> to endure the terrible sight without a trace of timidity
> and, at the moment of the meeting, to feel his strength
> so increased that he can undertake fully conscious the
> responsibility for transforming and beautifying the
> Guardian. (Ch. 10).

Transformation

The task of transforming the lower members of man's being into higher ones begins with the transformation of the astral body into the 'spirit self'. This higher self is free from the influences of Lucifer and Ahriman, who contribute so much to our experience of our lower self.

In working on the lower self, the I does not erase it, but transforms the raw materials it offers. Facing this task gives us the opportunity of observing our soul as it moves between Lucifer and Ahriman. When we long to be free of the problems that beset us and grow impatient with our slow progress, we are falling prey to a fantasy of escape. If on the other hand we grow depressed and decide that we are condemned forever to be the victim of our problems, we have given in to the spirit who denies freedom. If we decide that we 'know' either of these to be true, our I has been drawn too far into the sphere of the soul. The I itself accepts our struggles and works with them creatively, as we might with a child – patiently but not indulgently, with a clear vision of wholeness and yet with understanding. Then we can be creative between the extremes. Once we manage to master some habit or tendency that we have grappled with for years it is transformed into a gift

114

of understanding. We have compassion for others who may still be grappling with this problem; our eyes are opened too for the work of the adversary powers that gave rise to this one-sidedness in ourselves.

The renewed capacity to find the middle between the extremes is bestowed by the Incarnation, through the seed-Word unfolding its life within us. The trajectory of development, which otherwise would have resulted in a divorce between earthly human beings and their divine source, is changed. The healing gift of the Incarnation is freely given. It is left to us to decide how we will make use of the renewed possibilities given to us.

Living with our souls in this way means that we practise being our own lawgiver. Freedom becomes a lived reality. Such freedom is not lack of constraint, or license. Rather it is freedom for great ends that we long to serve as human beings. Whenever we work to serve a purpose, we freely choose to limit our freedom. Accountability to a purpose is a law that we have given ourselves. This is reflected in the following quotation by Rudolf Steiner:

> At first man was to be given the Law from above. The Law of one's own I could however, only become what it was to be, when that I takes into itself the great Prototype of Golgotha, saying: 'If I take into my soul such thinking as was thought by the Being Who offered Himself in sacrifice on Golgotha, if I take into myself such feelings as were felt by the Being Who offered Himself as sacrifice on Golgotha, if I take into myself such willing as was willed by the Being Who offered Himself in sacrifice on Golgotha, then will my being come to a decision within itself to develop increasingly a likeness to God, it will then no longer have to follow the Outer Law, the Ten Commandments, but an inner impulse, its own Law.' *(The Christ Impulse,* Feb 2, 1910).

Outreach

The seed-Word was sown in our souls in order that it can germinate in us, bear fruit and multiply. From the beginning, those who experienced Christ communicated their experience. Jesus Christ sent his disciples out to prepare towns and villages for his arrival. At Whitsun, the Apostles felt compelled to spread the good news about what they had experienced. Christianity was never supposed to remain the secret property of a small group. In this sense, it is a missionary religion.

When we recognise that Christ is now at work in every human being who is struggling to find his or her true self, the meaning of mission is changed. We do not need to ask people 'have you been saved?' or 'do you have a personal relationship with Jesus Christ?' as if he were a stranger that they should get to know. Rather, we need to find the question that will unlock their experiences. We become less concerned with *telling* and more with *asking*. We will start to collect our own 'gospel' – the countless stories of Christ coming to life in human souls, such as Ed's story (pp. 110f). These are the stories for which the whole world would not have space, if they were all written down (as is said in John 21:25)

If Christ is already there deep within every human being, we could ask whether we ever need to mention his name, which often closes doors in a conversation. Does it make a difference to know his name, if someone experiences him as the power of resurrection in their hour of darkness, or as the one who unites them with all other human beings on earth?

We only have to read the newspaper or turn on the radio to find an answer to this. Our culture has largely rejected traditional religion. We have seen that this is a necessary part of our journey towards freedom. However, the replacement is morally and spiritually corrosive. Where religion used to provide a horizon that lifted many people's gaze beyond the satisfaction of their animal needs, what has replaced it to a large extent in mass culture is entertainment and consumerism. For many people, the only thing that transcends daily concerns is family. Family bonds are indeed precious, but they crack under the strain if they are made to bear the whole burden of human beings' need to feel that we are part of something greater than ourselves.

In intellectual life, evolutionary biology is seen to have supplied the explanations for human origins and to have replaced any moral code. A particularly potent venom is reserved for those who dare to talk about meaning, let alone Christ, in the liberal media. Occasionally, people committed to a secular society ponder where the ethical values will come from in a world without God. What dogmatic religion has to offer is not considered as a possible source. There are voices that are aware that there is no future for a society that denies the deepest well-spring of its true being. Oliver James' book *Affluenza* is only one of many testimonies to the corrosiveness of consumer culture. It is hard to envisage where renewal could come from, if the spiritual life is excluded; hard too to imagine humanity accepting guidance from the old guardians of the spiritual life.

Since the fourth century, the spiritual world was progressively banished to a separate realm of existence. Starting in the fifteenth century and gathering pace ever since, the human spirit has rejected the dogma that the only true glory was to be found in a world far away. This opened the way for our experiences in a world that had forsaken the gods. The lonely self, thrown back upon itself, turns out to be the place where the immortal diamond that was the gift of the Incarnation is formed. This is the experience of countless human beings.

Merely feeling this reality does not represent the end of the path. As we saw in Chapter 1, the circle is closed when the seed-Word within us helps us to recognise the Word outside of us. When we know the name of the one who made this experience possible, we can direct our lives towards this experience, and communicate it to others. We can name the forces that would reduce human life to a merely animal level and counterbalance them. We can take up our roles as co-creators of a truly human culture – one which embraces all the dimensions of existence.

→ *Contemplation on Christ* ←

This contemplation introduces a text by Rudolf Steiner in which he shows how we can allow a spiritual reality to come to life within us.

When we face the physical Sun and receive from it warmth and light we know that we are living in a reality. In the same way we must live in the presence of Christ, the spiritual Sun, who has joined His life to that of the Earth, and receive actively from Him into our souls that which in the spiritual world corresponds to warmth and light. We will feel ourselves permeated by 'spiritual warmth' when we experience the 'Christ in me.' Feeling ourselves thus permeated we will say to ourselves:

'This warmth liberates my humanity from the bonds of the Cosmos in which it may not remain. For me to gain my freedom the Divine-Spiritual Being of primeval times had to lead me into regions where it could not remain with me, where, however, it gave me Christ, that His forces might bestow upon me as a free human being what the Divine-Spiritual primeval Being once gave me by way of Nature, which was then also the Spirit-way. This warmth leads me back again to the divine sources, whence I came.'

And in this feeling there will grow within us, in inner warmth of soul, the experience in and with Christ and the experience of real and true humanity. 'Christ gives me my humanity' – that will be the fundamental feeling which will well up in the soul and pervade it. (*Anthroposophical Leading Thoughts,* from Michael's Mission in the Cosmic Age of Human Freedom)

This beautiful passage resounds all the more strongly when we prepare the space in our soul. As we read the first sentence, we could think of experiences of the warmth of the sun, its generous abundance when we were in a hot country;

or as a contrast, experiences of cold, when we longed for the sun, and our joy when we felt its warmth again. Similarly, we could relate the sentences on freedom to the final chapter of the book and to the transition from obedience to outer law to inner law. Each sentence can be prepared in this way. The more we have worked with the text, the richer the sounding space for it will be in our soul.

We could use the sentence 'Christ gives me my humanity' to meditate on. We could then read the other sentences slowly through, filling them with the images and experiences we have prepared. We allow all of that to live in our soul, and then to fade away. Then we hear the words resounding: 'Christ gives me my humanity.'

Glossary

Arius Priest in Alexandria, lived 250 or 256–336. Became famous in the debate about the nature of the Divine Word. See p. 31.

Athanasius Priest and later Bishop of Alexandria, lived 296–373. See p. 32.

Christology The theological discipline that studies the person and work of Jesus Christ.

Constantine Lived c. 272–337, Emperor 306–37. Sometimes called the Great, or Saint Constantine. He was the first Roman Emperor openly to favour the Church, and was baptised on his deathbed.

Consubstantial (Greek: *homoousion*) means 'of the same nature or substance'.

Council of Nicaea 325. Called by the Roman Emperor Constantine to address some divisions in the Church, the most important of which was the Arian dispute. Well over 300 bishops attended, representing the whole Church, though the overwhelming majority were from the Greek-speaking East. See pp. 30ff.

Council of Chalcedon 451. Held at the behest of the Emperor Marcian with the intention of bringing the disputes about the two natures in Jesus Christ to an end.

Cyril of Alexandria Lived 378–444; Bishop 412–44. Opponent of Nestorius and proponent of the idea of the human and the divine being a single nature after the union in Jesus Christ.

Docetism Umbrella term for teachings that deny the reality of the humanity of Christ. Because God is so utterly different to anything in the sense-world, he could only appear as a man, but he could never become human. God cannot die on the cross.

Ebionite Umbrella term for teachings that deny the divinity of Jesus Christ. Mainly found in the Holy Land in the first century.

Etheric body Rudolf Steiner uses the word etheric to describe those forces at work in nature and in the human being which raise the forces at work to a level beyond the merely physical. The etheric body is a contained field of these forces.

Gregory of Nazianzus (c. 329–89). Originally a pupil of Apollinaris, he spoke out against him in the debate about the human nature in Jesus Christ.

Hierarchies The three ranks of respectively three angelic beings described in ancient mysticism and theology on whom Rudolf Steiner casts new light. Their names are, starting nearest to human beings, and using the terms usually used in this book: Angels, Archangels, Archai; Spirits of Form (Exousiai), Spirits of Movement (Dynameis), Spirits of Wisdom (Kyriotetes); Thrones, Cherubim and Seraphim.

Hopkins, Gerard Manley (1844–89) English poet. He converted to Catholicism and became a Jesuit in 1870. Hardly any of his poetry was published in his lifetime, and it only survived because his friend, Robert Bridges, saved the copies Hopkins sent him and published them after his death.

Hypostasis In the Christological debates of the fourth and fifth centuries, hypostasis was used in contrast to ousia. Ousia is the underlying nature of a thing, hypostasis means a particular instance.

Incarnation literally means 'enfleshment'. It refers to John 1:14, 'And the Word became flesh and dwelt among us.' The very starkness of the term 'flesh' draws attention to the reality of the union between the divine and human worlds.

Justin Martyr (100–165). One of the first generation of Christian thinkers, usually called Apologists, Justin sought a synthesis between Christian faith and Greek philosophy. In this context, apology means a defence of Christianity.

Logos or Word. Term from Greek philosophy meaning the creative principle, also reason. Christian thinkers such as Justin Martyr saw in the concept of the Logos the key to understanding the identity of Jesus Christ.

Modalism The belief that God is one person who reveals himself in three forms or modes, the opposite extreme to Tritheism. Modalism (also called Sabellianism) was condemned as a heresy by Dionysius, Bishop of Rome, in 262.

Nestorius (c. 386–450), Bishop of Constantinople 428–31. Most famous or notorious representative of the school of thought loosely grouped around Antioch. He emphasised the full human nature in Jesus Christ. Out-manoeuvred and exiled by Cyril of Alexandria.

Origen (184/5–253/4) Leader of the Catechumen School in Alexandria for many years, he was the author of the first systematic theology, his On First Principles, which drew on Scripture, reason and mystery-wisdom to put together a picture of Creation, earthly existence and Salvation.

Ousia See hypostasis.

Steiner, Rudolf (1861–1925) Steiner was a researcher and teacher of what he called Spiritual Science, which rests on the conviction that the things and beings of the spiritual world can be known as clearly as those of the sense-perceptible world.

Tritheism The belief in three separate and distinct gods: Father, Son and Holy Spirit, as opposed to monotheism, the belief in one God. In trinitarian monotheism, three divine persons are seen within the one divine nature.

Bibliography

Athanasius, *De Incarnatione,* www.ccel.org/ccel/schaff/npnf204.vii.i.html

Bock, Emil, *The Three Years,* Floris Books, Edinburgh 2005.

—, *The Apocalypse of Saint John,* Floris Books, Edinburgh 2005.

Boom, Corrie ten, *The Hiding Place,* Hachette, London 2012.

Catechism of the Catholic Church, www.vatican.va/archive/ENG0015/_INDEX.HTM.

Constantine, *Letter to Bishop Alexander,* www.fourthcentury.com/urkunde-17/.

Frend, W. H. *Creeds, Councils and Controversies,* SPCK, Cambridge 1989.

Gregory Nazianzen, *To Cledonius the Priest Against Apollinarius. (Ep. Cl.)* www.ccel.org/ccel/schaff/npnf207.iv.ii.iii.html

Henderson, Ruth, *Empathy and the Disturbing Power of Forgiveness* people.bu.edu/rhh/proteus.html

Hopkins, Gerard Manley, The Poems of Gerard Manley Hopkins (ed. Gardner et al), Oxford University Press 1970.

Irenaeus, *Against Heresies,* www.newadvent.org/fathers/0103.htm.

James, Oliver, *Affluenza,* Vermillion, London 2007.

Justin Martyr, *Dialogue with Trypho,* www.earlychristianwritings.com/text/justinmartyr-dialoguetrypho.html.

Kelly, J.N.D. *Early Christian Doctrines,* A & C Black, London 1985.

Lewis, C.S. *The Magician's Nephew,* HarperCollins, London 2001.

McQuarrie, *Jesus Christ in Modern Thought,* SCM Press, London, 1990.

Moore, Sebastian, *Jesus the Liberator of Desire,* Crossroad, London 1989.

New Scientist Magazine, online special on the self. www.newscientist.com/special/self.

Origen: *On First Principles,* www.ccel.org/ccel/schaff/anf04.vi.v.html

Shepherd, Canon A.J. *The Battle for the Spirit – The Church and Rudolf Steiner,* Anastasis, Weobley 1994.

—, *Rudolf Steiner: Scientist of the Invisible,* Floris, Edinburgh 1983.

Steiner, Rudolf. Volume Nos refer to the Collected Works (CW), or to the German Gesamtausgabe (GA).

—, *According to Luke: The Gospel of Compassion and Love Revealed* (CW 114) Anthroposophic Press, USA 2001.

—, *Anthroposophical Leading Thoughts* (CW 26) Rudolf Steiner Press, UK 1998.

—, *Building Stones for an Understanding of the Mystery of Golgotha* (CW 175) Rudolf Steiner Press, UK 1972.

—, *Christ and the Twentieth Century* (CW 60) Anthroposophic Press, USA 1971.

—, *The Christ Impulse and the Development of the Ego-Consciousness* (CW 116) Anthroposophic Press, USA 1976.

—, *The Christian Mystery* (CW 97) Completion Press, Australia 2007.

—, *The Fifth Gospel: From the Akashic Record* (CW 148) Rudolf Steiner Press, UK 1998.

—, *From Beetroot to Buddhism* (CW 353) Rudolf Steiner Press, UK 1999.

—, *From Jesus to Christ* (CW 131) Rudolf Steiner Press, UK 2005.

—, *Die Geistige Vereinigung der Menschheit durch den Christus-Impuls* (GA 165) Dornach 2006.

—, *The Gospel of St John and its Relation to the Other Gospels* (CW 112) Anthroposophic Press, USA 1983.

—, *How to Know Higher Worlds: A Modern Path of Initiation* (CW 10) Anthroposophic Press, USA 1994 (also translated as *Knowledge of the Higher Worlds: How is it Achieved?*).

—, *Inner Experiences of Evolution* (CW 132) SteinerBooks, USA 2008.

—, *Intuitive Thinking as a Spiritual Path: A Philosophy of Freedom* (CW 4) Anthroposophic Press, USA 1995 (also translated as *The Philosophy of Freedom* and as *The Philosophy of Spiritual Activity*).

—, *Knowledge of the Higher Worlds: How is it Achieved?* (CW 10) Rudolf Steiner Press, UK 2009 (also translated as *How to Know Higher Worlds*).

—, *Die menschliche Seele in ihrem Zusammenhang mit göttlich geistigen Individualitäten* (GA 224) Dornach 1983.

—, *The Mystery of the Trinity* (CW 214) Rudolf Steiner Publishing Co, UK 1947.

—, *Occult Science: an Outline* (CW 13) Rudolf Steiner Press, UK 2013 (also translated as *an Outline of Esoteric Science*).

—, *An Outline of Esoteric Science* (CW 13) Anthroposophic Press, USA 1997 (also translated as *Occult Science: an Outline*).

—, *The Philosophy of Freedom: The Basis for a Modern World Conception* (CW 4) Rudolf Steiner Press, UK 2011 (also translated as *The Philosophy of Spiritual Activity* and as *Intuitive Thinking as a Spiritual Path*).

—, *The Philosophy of Spiritual Activity* (CW 4) SteinerBooks, USA 2007 (also translated as *The Philosophy of Freedom* and as *Intuitive Thinking as a Spiritual Path*).

—, *The Reappearance of Christ in the Etheric* (CW 118) Anthroposophic Press, USA 2004.

—, *The Spiritual Hierarchies and the Physical World* (CW 110) SteinerBooks, USA 2008.

—, *Theosophy: An Introduction to the Spiritual Processes in Human Life and in the Cosmos* (CW 9) Anthroposophic Press, USA 1994.

—, *The Waking of the Human Soul and the Forming of Destiny* (CW 224) Steiner Book Centre, Vancouver 1983.

—, *The World of the Senses and the World of the Spirit* (CW 134) Anthroposophic Press, USA 1979.

Taylor, John, *The Go-Between God,* SCM, London 1972.

Tutu, Desmond, 'Desmond Tutu on Nelson Mandela: "Prison became a crucible"' www.theguardian.com/commentisfree/2013/dec/06/desmond-tutu-nelson-mandela.

Williamson, Marianne, *A Return to Love: Reflections on the Principles of "A Course in Miracles",* HarperCollins, 1992.

Young, Frances, *The Making of the Creeds,* SCM, Bury St Edmunds 2002.

Zajonc, Arthur, *Meditation as Contemplative Enquiry,* Lindisfarne USA 2008.

Index

You may also be interested in

The Christian Community is a religious movement which draws on the help and inspiration of Rudolf Steiner. One way in which it differs from other churches is that it does not demand adherence to any creed or view of the world from its members.

Nevertheless, spiritual, philosophical and religious questions arise, and by thinking about and discussing them, members can become part of the spiritual conversation that has been underway for the last two thousand years, since human beings have grappled to understand what they experience in Jesus Christ.

This book, the first of its kind to explore the theology of The Christian Community in a systematic way, asks such questions and offers many insights into religious life and experience. In the first half, Tom Ravetz addresses questions about God, the Trinity, the Incarnation, the Holy Spirit and evil. In the second half, he traces humanity's journey from oneness, to multiplicity, and to a new oneness through community.

florisbooks.co.uk